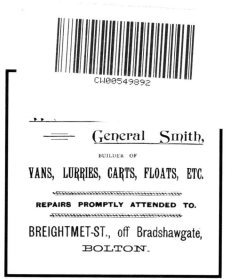

The Beginnings in Bolton

A form of mechanically operated road transport appeared in Bolton in October 1847, when Arthur Farries of Preston demonstrated his patent self-propelled omnibus outside the Temperance Hall on St Georges Road. The Bolton Chronicle stated this 'Wonderful Travelling Machine' could convey twelve passengers at 10mph 'without the aid of either Steam or Horses'.

The means of propulsion were, in fact, the driver's legs. He operated a treadmill connected to a form of gearbox with no fewer than 24 ratios and steering was by a tiller and chains connected to a standard wagon centre-swivelling axle. This 'wonderful' device soon disappeared into the realms of history.

Steam traction engines were regulated under the Highways Acts of 1861 and 1865. These decreed that engines must observe speed limits of 4mph in the country and 2mph in towns, as well as any local byelaws. Three attendants were compulsory; two on the engine and one to precede on foot 60 yards ahead, carrying a red flag in daytime or a red lamp at night. They must stop immediately in the vicinity of horses. An Amendment in 1878 reduced the distance to 20 yards and the red flag or lamp was no longer required, although local authorities could demand their continued use.

On 31st August 1872 the Bolton Chronicle reported that a traction engine and two trailers had been used on a works outing to Rivington from Messrs Pollitt's Rose Hill boiler works.

Eighty workmen left Bolton at 1.30pm and arrived at the picnic site at 4.30pm. The steam whistle was sounded for recall about 7.00pm and about 11.00pm the engine and trailers reached the lower end of Chorley New Road, where wives and girlfriends were waiting and 'managed to obtain a lift back to town'. The paper noted that a speed of 8mph had been reached - double the permitted limit.

In December 1874 Richard Pollitt, boilermaker, was charged with allowing his traction engine to travel without a person in front with a red flag. The court was told that the engine had been travelling towards Bury and when it had trouble climbing the hill at Tonge Fold, owing to ice on the road, the man in front had gone to help the driver. The court awarded a Caution Note and fined Mr Pollitt £2.

Another Pollitt 'established 1846' in the transport industry and having to adapt to changing times by 1896

As the use of traction engines became more widespread, more regulations were introduced and on 2nd June 1883 the Bolton Journal reported that George Carter of Wigan had been fined under a new Bolton Corporation byelaw concerning steam engines travelling along the borough's highways. They were prohibited from the town between 9.00am and 5.00pm and Mr Carter had been driving along Deansgate at one in the afternoon. This was an example of the punitive legislation against mechanically propelled vehicles on public roads in the nineteenth century. But, in fairness to Bolton Corporation, it was no doubt prompted by concern for road surfaces and horse transport.

Under the Act of 1861 every mechanically propelled vehicle used for haulage on public roads had to be licensed by the local authority in whose area it operated. If it was entering another district, prior permission had to be obtained and a fee paid on a daily basis. This rule doesn't seem to have been enforced in Bolton, and it was not until October 1902 that the Streets Committee resolved that no traction engine or similar vehicle would be allowed to enter the borough without a permit.

It was also agreed that the Town Clerk and Borough Engineer would consider a report of road damage caused by traction engines. That this matter had been finally settled is made clear in a Bolton Evening News report of 5th January 1903. John Miller of Darwen was fined

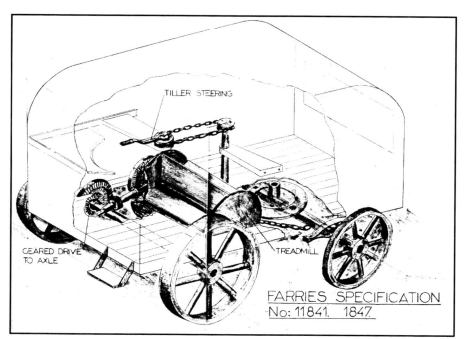

TILLER STEERING

GEARED DRIVE TO AXLE

TREADMILL

FARRIES SPECIFICATION
No: 11841. 1847

The omnibus designed by Arthur Farries of Preston and shown in Bolton in 1847

15/- and costs for operating his traction engine in Hacken Lane without paying the 2/6d for a daily permit. The permit system must have been somewhat cumbersome to enforce and the byelaw was no doubt broken on many occasions.

In February 1896 Messrs Deakins, dyers and bleachers of Belmont, were accused by Astley Bridge District Council of damaging roads in their jurisdiction. Two years later the firm was taken to court on similar charges. Undeterred, in 1899 Deakins experimented with a different form of road transport, beginning regular trips from Belmont to warehouses in Manchester with two Leyland steam lorries.

The 18-mile run had always proved difficult for horses, owing to the elevated position of Belmont. The steam lorry, with a load of four tons, made the trip in about four hours. The Manchester Evening News commented: 'So far the experiment has proved effective. The presence of the motor lorry in Manchester has caused some excitement, motor vehicles are not uncommon nowadays but this, we understand, is the first motor lorry. A speed of 8mph can be obtained with ease on the country roads.'

The official report of the trials states that the prime cost of a Leyland was £375 and the annual expenditure based on a 35-mile day was £367.12s.9d. Following the 1904 Heavy Motor Car Act, Deakins' two steamers were registered BN25 and BN26.

There was an early motor car visitor to Bolton in 1894, when a Lutzmann arrived to advertise Mother Shipton's soap. Friedrich Lutzmann, a leading pioneer of the car in Germany, made his first car in 1893 and in 1898 sold his design to Adam Opel's son, who produced the car at Russelsheim as 'System Lutzmann'.

Motor cars are mentioned in a short article in a supplement to the Bolton Journal & Guardian of 26th October 1895, which included the prophetic statement that the horseless carriage was 'the vehicle of the future'. The following year, on the occasion of the Crystal Palace Motor Show, a Journal reporter wrote that the Exhibition 'may have far-reaching consequences to more than one trade in this country, and will certainly tend to largely alter our national system of locomotion.'

The first time motor cars came to Bolton in any number was on Monday 30th April 1900, when 54 vehicles passed through the town between 7 and 8 o'clock in the morning, during the Automobile Club of Great Britain's 1,000-mile London to Edinburgh and return trial.

A Bolton Chronicle reporter travelled with the cavalcade from Manchester to Kendal in a car driven by Maurice Edwards (founder of Edbro Ltd), and provided by H Cooper & Co, cycle makers of 109 Bradshawgate and 6 Great Moor Street. Cooper & Co, according to the reporter, 'had for some time been pushing the motor trade and made, under Butler Patents, the 2hp quadri-cycle.'

After the ride to Kendal the reporter noted that the car was 'an excellent mount'. Taking advantage of this, Cooper & Co advertised 'Cycles, Velocipedes and Motors' in the Journal of 2nd June. It was Bolton's first motor advert. At the time there was a considerable number of cycle makers and dealers in the town and it was from this industry that the motor trade gradually developed.

On 10th December 1895 Sir David Salomons, Director of the South-Eastern Railway and enthusiastic pioneer motorist, presided over a meeting in London which led to the formation of the Self-Propelled Traffic Association. A Liverpool branch was formed a year later, with Lord Derby as President, and between 1898 and 1901 they organised competitive trials of motor vehicles.

A lady with her Edwardian motor-cycle. It had a single, air-cooled cylinder and string webbing from the rear mudguard to the belt-driven rear wheel hub to protect her skirt from burning on the exhaust pipe or catching in the belt

The 1901 trials included two motor lorries, entered by George F Milnes of London; these were the first petrol-engined commercial vehicles to come to Bolton. The engines were by Daimler, the chassis and transmission by Marienfeldt of Berlin (a company taken over by Daimler in 1902) and the bodies were built by Milnes. On 5th June 1901 they were part of a cavalcade of lorries and cars which arrived in a crowded Victoria Square to be greeted by the Mayor, Alderman Scowcroft, and other dignitaries.

The Bolton Journal reporter noted 'the steady, not to say graceful, way in which sharp curves round street corners were traversed.' The petrol vehicles were 'not by any means free from vibration,' and generally there was 'a strong smell of oil about.' This did not deter Aldermen Tong and Kearsley, together with the Borough Engineer, Mr Morgan, from accepting an invitation to ride in one of the private cars as far as St Helens in order to observe the lorries' performance more closely.

As far as Bolton was concerned, many witnesses thought that the motor vehicle was here to stay and that before long horse traction would be superseded by this new mode of transport.

Road Vehicle Registration and Garages in Bolton

The Motor Car Act of 1903, which dealt with the registration, licensing and taxation of motor vehicles, together with various speed limits, was the basis of our present-day system of driver and vehicle legislation.

The fundamental aspects of these laws did not come about overnight, and the pages of the Bolton Evening News give some idea of the scale and tenor of the debates. The edition of 16th May 1901 reported a meeting in London of County Council representatives to discuss 'Roads in relation to motor-cars and traction engines.'

Alderman W W B Hulton, Chair of the Lancashire County Council Main Roads & Bridges Committee, said his Council had 1,500 miles of public roads to administer. On the topic of motor cars he was of the opinion that, 'The sole object of drivers seemed to be to cover the ground as quickly as possible to show how perfect the machinery was,' and, 'Enjoying the scenery was out of the question; driving horses was becoming intolerable.' But he would not care to see motor cars 'disfigured by having to carry a

large number plate even though he was not a car owner himself.'

Alderman Hulton must have been suitably impressed by the motor car; on 7th June the Bolton Evening News reported that he was among the 100 representatives of County Councils at a motor car trial at Richmond Park, London. A few days earlier, at an Automobile Club luncheon, he proposed the toast to the Chairman, Lord Llangattock (the father of C S Rolls) and said that his Committee was not antagonistic to the new motor industry. Perhaps he was influenced by his admission that he was now a satisfied owner of an electric car.

On 31st January 1902 the Bolton Evening News reported on a meeting between the County Councils Association and Walter Long, President of the Board of Trade, regarding the regulation of motor cars. On the subject of speed limits, Alderman Hulton said the Main Roads Committee had considered a 4mph limit on certain roads, but generally favoured 12mph. As for the easy identification of motor cars, he hoped that Mr Long 'would

One of the two Milnes-Daimler lorries which was part of the cavalcade of 13 vehicles in Bolton on 5th June 1901

consider that the crest or coronet on the carriage and livery of its owner was sufficient means of identification within 6-10 miles of the permanent residence of the owner, and that if it was considered necessary to have some mark then it should not be conspicuous but so placed that a police constable could get at the information that he may require.'

In June 1903 Mr G Harwood, MP for Bolton, admitted in the House of Commons to a fascination with motor cars and said that he had in fact travelled at 30mph in one. He was of the opinion that they should carry a number and Mr Long said the Government recognised the need for 'fresh legislation,' as the present state could not remain.

The Bolton Evening News of 8th July reported that Lord Balfour had presented the new Motor Car Bill to Parliament. Cars should be registered by county councils and bear distinguishing marks and a number. Anyone who drove a motor car for hire should be licensed and the 12mph maximum speed permitted under the 1896 Act should be maintained in urban district council areas.

On 31st July the Bolton Evening News quoted a reply from Mr Long to a critic of the Motor Car Bill. He said that it was his conviction of the inability of the Law to protect ordinary users of the highways which had induced him to introduce the Bill, which had, 'with careful, and even anxious, forethought, been devised to strengthen the Law in the very interests of quiet, reasonable, middle-class people.'

During the first half of 1903 Alderman Hulton had authorised a traffic survey which showed that from 12th February to 11th June, 798 single journeys were made by motor wagons over main roads from Blackburn and Darwen to Bolton. On the Preston to Blackburn road, 109 journeys were recorded in one week in June. The fact that road surfaces were being subjected to an ever-increasing weight of traffic was causing great concern.

The new Bill made no reference to motor wagons and it was strongly urged that with all motor cars and wagons plying for hire, the laden, rather than unladen, weight should be the criterion and that speeds should be restricted accordingly to prevent, as far as possible, road disintegration. The width of the tyre should be proportional to the weight of the vehicle. (Most vehicles in the class would have been fitted with iron-tyred, cart-type wheels.)

Replying to a correspondent in the middle of August, Mr Long said that he hoped the Bill would divert car makers 'from the construction of costly racing machines beyond the reach of all but millionaires,' to 'modestly-sized vehicles adapted to the purse of the man of moderate means,' and ended with, 'The Bill will penalise the speed merchants.'

Public notices were issued requiring owners of motor cars and motor cycles to register with the Watch Committee and on 31st December the Bolton Evening News reported that between 18th and 29th of the month, 17 motor cars and 22 motor cycles had been registered. 35 licences to drive had been issued and for an annual fee of £3, dealers in vehicles had been issued with

two numbers (the forerunners of trade plates) to enable them to demonstrate their wares on the roads.

The Motor Car Act became law on 1st January 1904, imposing speed limits of 20mph on highways and 10mph in towns, but, according to the Bolton Evening News, 'locally it is not proposed at present to exercise authority in this respect. The motorist, in a word, is on trial for his good behaviour.' The situation in Leigh was quite different, for their Watch Committee decided on the 10mph limit in towns. Thus someone from Bolton could, unwittingly, find themselves breaking the law as soon as they entered the town. To add to the confusion, Farnworth took the same decision as Leigh.

On 13th January the Bolton Evening News listed the numbers of car and motor cycle registrations and drivers' licences issued for various towns and cities in the North. The figures included 22 registrations and 23 licences in Blackburn, 225 and 231 in Liverpool, 353 and 363 in Manchester, 40 and 52 in Preston and 24 and 16 in Wigan. The Motor Car Act also allocated prefix letters to those

Even in big cities like Liverpool, horse transport still dominated, but things were changing rapidly, as this early 20th century advert shows

authorised to license motor vehicles. Bolton was BN, Lancashire County Council B, Blackburn CB, Bury EN, Manchester N, Liverpool K, Preston CK and Salford BA. The letters were followed by up to four digits.

Vehicles other than cars and motor cycles came under the Heavy Motor Car Order of December 1904. A 'heavy' vehicle was one whose unladen weight exceeded two tons and the maximum permitted speed was 8mph, or 5mph if pulling a trailer. The cost of registration was £10 for up to 10 tons unladen, plus £2 for every ton or fraction over. For regular travel to another borough or county council area, a further £5 was charged. If such visits were only occasional, the charge was 2/6d a day.

This type of vehicle was usually steam driven and ran on steel treaded wheels. If the wheels had pneumatic or solid rubber tyres, the speed limit was raised to 12mph for up to 6 tons registered axle weight and 8mph above this.

Between 1903 and 1921, 45 garages, traders or vehicle operators in Bolton were issued with trade numbers, which indicates the extent of the motor trade here in the early part of the century. Trade numbers were issued before 1914 to:

Bolton Motor Co, 121-123 St Georges Road (December 1903)

James Veoux Madgwick, 79 Knowsley Street (December 1903)

Bolton Automobile & Steam Wagon Works (John Robinson Tate & Frank Tate), 57 All Saints St (January 1904)

Bolton Motor Wagon Co (J Bradshaw & Sons), Turk St (January 1904)

William Brimelow, 111 Manchester Road (March 1904)

Thomas Fitton & James Henry Green, Central Motor Co, 82 Victoria Square (December 1904)

Carlton Motor Co (Isaiah Dootson), Carlton Street, 17 Bridgeman Place (February 1905)

Central Motor Co, 82 Victoria Square (owned by William Harris Hall, 684 Bury Road, Breightmet; James Battersby, Wyresdale Road; Thomas & George Temperley, 'Louisville', Albert Road) (February 1907)

Stanley Parker, Roe Buck Hotel, Kay Street; Stanley Motor Garage, Westbrook Street (February 1911)

Richard Pilkington, 65 Hilden Street Manchester Bros, St Georges Road (June 1911)

Lewis Merrall & Bernard Brown, 56 Bridge Street (October 1911) and Premier Motor Works 119-123 St Georges Road (February 1913)

The Grosvenor Motor Co, Bradford Street West (July 1912)

William Grundy, 169a Bradshawgate (February 1913)

Henry Spragg & James Hodkinson, Victoria Garage, Tonge Moor Road (February 1913)

William, Charles, Maurice and Miles Edwards, Parkfield Garage, Dawes Street (March 1913)

Bolton Garage Ltd, Byng Street East (February 1914)

Albert Seymour Ryan, 159 Bradshawgate (February 1914)

Ernest Townson (Townson & Chadwick) (February 1914)

James Demosthenes Brookes, 'The Nook', St Michaels Avenue, Great Lever (March 1914) (estate agent)

William Henry, Isabel and Wilfred Vernon Legat, trading as W H Legat, Son & Co, 'Cross Axes', St Georges Street, and 108-110 Great Moor Street (April 1914)

Bolton's first registration, BN1, was allocated to Joseph Magee of Magee

Registration number BN196 on Higher Bridge Street - a 16hp Humber owned by Mr T W Shaw of Astley Bridge

Marshall Ltd, brewers, for a 15hp Panhard-Levassor.

Registration books for the BN series show that a further 35 vehicles were registered by the end of January 1904, and by the end of the year the total had reached 89. The list of vehicles shows a remarkable cross-section of makes:

Cars: Panhard, Benz, Belsize, Daimler, New Orleans, Talbot, Decauville, De Dion, Georges-Richard, Swift, Peugeot, Vulcan, Coventry-Motet, Clement, MMC, Progress, Lanchester, Wolseley.

Motor cycles: Kerry, Minerva, Triumph, Ormond, Eagle, Norton, Raleigh, Rex, Clyde, Camillo, Royal Ruby, Humber, Mayflower, Brown, Excelsior, Phoenix, Whitworth, Reliance, Deane-Rapid, Centaur, De Dion.

Steamer lorries: Yorkshire Patent, Thornycroft, Entwisle & Gass (Bolton), Coulthard, Leyland, Bolton Motor Wagon Co.

Steamer cars: Gardner-Serpollet, Locomobile.

Shortly before the onset of World War One in August 1914 the registration of motor vehicles by Bolton Corporation had reached BN1634; (a random selection is shown in the table, right.)

Numbers grew steadily and by the time the Bolton Motor Taxation Office opened in 1921, there were 3,363 locally registered vehicles on the books.

The last of the BN registration series, BN9999, was issued in May 1927 and was for a charabanc owned by J R Tognarelli. Bolton's second prefix, WH, lasted until 1938, when the first of the three letter prefixes, ABN appeared. WH1 was allocated to the mayoral car.

BN115 3.5hp Benz John Dennis Bates, Prospect House, Harwood 23 June 1904

BN130 10hp Decauville. Isaiah Dootson, Spring Lane, Heaton. 15 July 1904

BN325 18hp White Steam car. Tom Jackson, 'Waterfoot', Heaton. 14 November 1906

BN537 16hp Vulcan. Edmund Holden, Clarence Yard, Bolton 12 March 1910

BN659 14/16hp Belsize. Percy Southern, Bolton 23 March 1911

BN1102 15hp Austin. Percy Southern, 343 Blackburn Road, Astley Bridge 4 February 1913

BN1634 10/12hp Belsize. Stanley and Arthur Manchester, St Georges Road. 4 June 1914

Pioneer Bolton motorist Mr Edward Hope, with his wife Susanna, sons Edward, Frank and Walter and daughter Edith, outside Haslam Park, Wigan Road, in their Vulcan BN101, registered 23rd April 1904

Early Petrol Regulation

In the 1860s it was suggested that petroleum and its products should be treated in a similar manner to gunpowder and made subject to similar storage conditions. As a result, the Petroleum Act of 1870 gave local watch committees the power to license premises for storage of this commodity, and issue fines for non-compliance. The first prosecution in Bolton under the Act was in June 1875. John Priestley, chemist of Deansgate, was summonsed for holding petroleum on his premises without a licence.

A licence was needed if over three gallons were stored and the oil had to be kept in one pint containers of glass, stone or earthenware. If more than three gallons were stored without a licence, a fine of £30 a day could be levied and the oil confiscated. Mr Priestley had half a gallon in a single container and not in a separate building as the law required. He was fined 5/-, as the judge was of the opinion that he had not wilfully contravened the Act, as he had never received notice of it from Bolton Corporation.

The Autocar magazine for April 1899 notes that a Bolton cycle and pioneer motor trader, James Veoux Madgwick, had arranged with Thomas Moscrop's oil works for them to stock Pratt's motor spirit to supply 'at a moment's notice'. It would seem this was given official Watch Committee approval in July 1900, when an unnamed application for the storage of 'Locomotive Petroleum' was acceded to. Moscrop's name appears in the minutes for 24th September 1902, when the firm was permitted to increase its petrol storage from 250 gallons to 350.

There was another early application to the Watch Committee in May 1901. Mr Madgwick was permitted to store a quantity of petrol in the yard at the rear of the Thomasson Gymnasium (next to Folds Road School and now the site of Gordon's Honda garage). By this time he was in charge of the gymnasium as well as running his cycle and motor business at the top of Knowsley Street.

A report to the Watch Committee for the year ending 1903 stated that 12 persons had been granted petrol licences and a further 13 had been notified that they could store petrol for private use. (Private owners were permitted to hold a stock of petrol at home, provided it was in an approved container and in a suitable brick outhouse, under a 1900 Amendment to the Petroleum Act.) On 8th December 1904 the Central Motor Company, Victoria Square, was permitted to store petrol for retail sale in a shed behind their garage, provided it was sealed in 2-gallon tins.

As petrol sales increased, the demand for greater quantities reached the point where wholesale dealing became viable. Thus in October 1908 the Anglo-American Oil Co was permitted to store 600 gallons in premises in Rupert Street, Great Lever.

This was quickly followed by the British Petroleum Co being allowed to store 1,000 gallons on premises in Ninehouse Lane; by September 1912 this was increased to 2,000 gallons.

In December 1916 their licence was transferred to the Shell Marketing Co who, in April 1919, were given permission to store 24,000 gallons in two underground tanks and 6,000 gallons in 2-gallon tins at a new depot adjoining the London & North Western Railway goods yard in Bridgeman Street.

Around this time motor spirit cost about 11d a gallon and was duty free. Duty was first imposed on 30th April 1909 and in 1911 the retail price of first-grade motor spirit was 1/- a gallon; commercial grade was 11d a gallon. The prices included 3d a gallon Excise Duty.

An attempt to provide an alternative supply of petrol was the subject of an advertisement in the Bolton Journal of 7th January 1910.

Bridgewater Collieries, Brackley Coke Works, Little Hulton, stated that motor fuel, at 11d per gallon in 2-gallon tins, 'From Lancashire Coal by Lancashire Labour' was available from the following agents: E Holden of Bradshawgate, G Graveson & Sons of Farnworth, W H Jackson of Walkden, W Gore of Atherton, W Wilson of Swinton and R Farr & Son of Tyldesley.

The first underground storage tank was approved by the Watch Committee in June 1913, allowing John Jackson & Son to store 330 gallons at their corn mill in Weston Street. The second was approved in February 1915, for the Bolton Co-op Society to store 1,000 gallons at their Kay Street Depot.

There was no reference to pumping-out equipment when these applications were granted and it

Petrol rapidly replaced steam as a means of propulsion, and by the time of the First World War Bolton motor lorries were in service on the continent, as this magazine picture shows

The Bolton Motoring Scene, 1901-1905

was not until January 1916, when J H Bromilow was allowed to store 700 gallons in an underground tank, that 'Bowser Pumping and Storage Plant' is mentioned. The tank had to be embedded in concrete, not less than 18 inches below ground level at his garage in Cooper Row, off the bottom of Bank Street.

At the same time, John A Walker, cotton merchant of Saville Street, was allowed similar equipment for 2,000 gallons.

These were quickly followed by a number of other firms in Bolton. Applications for either 2,000 or 1,000 gallons storage were granted to Walker's Tannery, Barlow & Jones of Egyptian Street Mill, J Dearden of Gibraltar Mill and Barlow & Jones's Albert Mill by July 1916.

The pumping equipment had been patented in 1913 by Silvanus Freelove Bowser of Fort Wayne, Indiana, USA. It comprised a hand-cranked suction pump above the tank and enabled petrol to be filtered and delivered in precise, metered amounts to the waiting vehicle.

The Bolton Evening News of 6th July 1901 printed a report from the medical journal, The Lancet, on the topic of 'Speed and Control of Motor Cars'. It was no doubt directed towards the growing motoring population and referred to accidents 'calculated to bring the motor car into disrepute.' All concerned were counselled to do their utmost to 'suppress furious driving.' The writer considered that, until cars had a track of their own, they should be under strict control. An invention for automatic speed and noise control, attached to the driving axle, was needed and it must be compulsory - anyone not using it should be fined. The writer did not wish to interfere with the new means of locomotion, but advances must not be made at the expense of public safety.

The following month the Bolton Evening News reported that a Daimler car with a trailer, driven by 'a Manchester gentleman' reversed into the front window of Madgwick's 'cycle, motor and

camera' shop at the top of Knowsley Street in an attempt to enter the back street. This would seem to be an early, if not the first, motor accident in the town.

A week later, the BEN carried its first box number advert for a mechanically propelled vehicle - a motor-tricycle (probably a De Dion) 'as good as new, 30mph, £28, very cheap.'

The 5th August 1901 Bolton Evening News records what appears to have been the first fatal road accident involving a Bolton motorist. Three-year-old Bertie Benson had been killed by a motor car driven by Henry Albert Hoy, Chief Engineer at the L&Y Works at Horwich and of 'Springfield', Bromley Cross. Police evidence agreed that the car was being driven at 12mph, even though other witnesses were of the opinion that 16mph was nearer the mark. A verdict of accidental death was recorded. Perhaps Mr Hoy made some form of recompense to the boy's parents.

Bromilow's garage in Bank Street about 1917. On the left is a Vulcan flatbed, then a motor cycle, a Milnes Daimler and a Sentinel steam lorry. The site is now an open car park

On 4th November 1901 the Bolton Evening News reported its first local speeding case. The offender was Thomas Herbert Thwaites of Watermillock, who was accused of having 'furiously driven a motor car' in Blackburn Road, Astley Bridge.

PC Plimmer, standing at the Lawsons Arms, had estimated the speed as 20mph, but counsel for Mr Thwaites said the car could only reach 18mph and at the time in question it was in a gear which would only allow 10mph. Despite this, Mr Thwaites was fined 10/- and costs. During the hearing it was stated that he had driven 'above 7,000' miles, which would make him one of Bolton's pioneer motorists.

Bolton's early motoring scene had a number of pioneer traders, and in James Veoux Madgwick it had an outspoken and enthusiastic sponsor of anything connected with motor vehicles. The Bolton directory of 1888 lists him as a gymnastic instructor and for many years he was the PT instructor to Bolton School (Boys Division) and the Principal of the Thomasson Gymnasium; he also taught PT at the Bolton Lads' Club.

This was the era of the cycle, and in March 1890 he advertised in the Bolton Journal: 'Now open. The Central Cycle Depot, 79 Knowsley Street.' He was the sole agent for 'the four Best Makers in the World - Humber, New Rapids, Hillman, Herbert and Cooper, and also Rudge. Repairs and Sundries at lowest prices. All the latest novelties.' No doubt with an eye to business, the following month he announced the formation of a new cycling club, with himself as Captain.

It was Madgwick's interest in cycling that created a good relationship with Swain & Philipson's, makers of an allegedly puncture-proof tyre. By 1901 they were making tyres for motor cars at their works in Telford Street, Horwich, and in November 1901 Madgwick drove a car fitted with Swain tyres to the Stanley Show in London. The car, an Ariel Quad, made in Birmingham, and the

Swain tyres were exhibited there for a few days.

Reporting on the show, the Bolton Evening News noted that besides cycles and motorcycles, 'most of the best known makes of autocars' were to be seen. A number of new features had appeared, including 'friction clutches and gear drives in place of belts.' The paper also remarked that a high grade cycle cost £26 and a similar range motor cycle £45.

The Bolton Evening News for 16th April 1903 carried an advert for the Swain tyre. It was 'made in the exact shape a true tyre assumes when fully inflated,' and it could be folded up and put into the pocket as there were 'no wires, thickened edges, bolts, screws, etc, to secure [to the rim].' It was 'easily fitted without special tools with no risks to hands or nails.' The price of this marvel was 15/-.

On 30th September 1903 the Bolton Evening News reported the death at the age of 53 of Walter H Swain at his home, 177 Belmont Road. He had recently retired as Managing Director of Swain Patents' Syndicate Ltd and his successor was his son Leonard, who had been associated with the company since its inception. The obituary notes that W H Swain had been married twice and left seven daughters and two sons, and he had been linked with the Philipsons of Astley Bridge in tyre making for some years. In June 1904, for reasons unknown, the works plant and equipment at Telford Street, plus the patent rights to tyre manufacture, were sold at auction. Thus this aspect of Bolton's motoring history disappeared.

December 1901 saw the first public motor car auction in Bolton. The Bolton Evening News reported that one Albert Holley, acting on

instructions 'from one of the largest Motor Car Manufacturers' would be selling the following at the Drill Hall on 11th December:

1. 3hp Benz Ideal car, new, wire wheels, solid tyres, Crypto gear (a form of epicyclic gearing).

2. Allard 4-seater dog-cart, 5hp horizontal engine, artillery wheels, pneumatic tyres, walnut body, belt drive.

3. Decauville 3hp, two cylinder air-cooled, 3 speeds, 'very fast'.

4. Star 4-seater, 3hp engine, tangent (spoked) wheels, pneumatic tyres, water-cooled, belt driven.

5. Benz 3hp, tangent spoked wheels, Connolly tyres, specially finished with leather cushions. 2 cars available.

6 Allard Voiturette, 2-seater, 3hp De Dion engine, 3 speeds and reverse gears, 'very fast and reliable'.

7. Allard Rapid, belt driven, pneumatic tyres.

8. Allard 4-seater dog-cart, 5hp horizontal engine, belt driven.

One of many motor-cycles popular in the early twentieth century; note the emphasis on hill climbing, particularly useful in Bolton

The cars were on view and for trial from 9.00am of the sale day and free tuition was given to each purchaser.

The commercial vehicle trials in the summer of 1901 had created some interest amongst local industrialists. In fact, at least six had operated a road vehicle prior to the trials. The Bolton Evening News of 16th December 1901 refers to the Leyland steamer trials by Messrs Deakins and trials by other traders, such as Slaters of Dunscar, Stotherts of Atherton and Hardcastles, bleachers.

The Motor-Haulage Co of Bolton and Manchester was formed after trials conducted by J V Madgwick and a Mr F G Barrow of Market Street, Bolton, which involved transporting loads of cotton between Stockport and Manchester for a Bollington firm. This haulage business suffered some financial setbacks but, according to the same newspaper, these were resolved by Mr Barrow, who now had 'a place under his supervision at Chorlton-on-Medlock where 18-20 steamers, 40-50 motor cars and cycles are stored.' The article ended with an invitation to 'contact the well known automobile expert Mr F G Barrow MIME or Mr Madgwick who also is one of the pioneers in Automobile matters.'

In March 1902 Mr Madgwick announced a 'Great crisis in the Cycle Trade' and offered cycles 'made for him by the Eadie Manuf Co Ltd' at £6.15s. He also invited readers of the Bolton Evening News to view the Raleigh motorcycle at Knowsley Street. The 'crisis' does not seem to have affected him, for in April 1902 he advised customers that business was being conducted 'as usual during alterations.' The alterations must have been completed by early May 1902, when he announced that he was the sole agent for Daimler and Ariel cars, and for Humber, Raleigh and Quadrant 'Motor-Bicycles'. The following August he advertised the 'Latest Minerva type, the whole operation of driving controlled by one lever only.' It was so simple that anyone could learn to drive in ten minutes and he would be pleased to

show 'the workings' to intending purchasers. If customers could not afford new cars, he had a number of 'high-grade second-hand machines' left.

Robinson's cycle dealers of Bath Street also underwent some alterations in 1902 and in May were advertising the Humber chain-driven motorcycle. It was not 'a motor hung on to an ordinary bicycle, but a specially built motor-bicycle with positive chain drive.'

The Bolton Evening News published regular articles on cycling matters by someone with the pen-name 'Rambler' and he made his first mention of motorcycles on 5th November 1902. He seemed to think that they were still generally unacceptable, but 'To many a business or professional man it has proved an unexpectedly economical instrument, besides being an expeditious mode of locomotion.' A lot of cycle agents were dabbling in the business, but 'Those who contemplate investing in this evidently exhilarating pastime should choose their agent cautiously, there isn't much change out of £50 when a good new motor-cycle is bought.'

Two weeks later Rambler had thrown caution to the winds and

related how he had 'sampled' a 2hp Centaur from Madgwick's and completed a trip round Yarrow Bridge and Rivington. He was of the opinion that an hour on a motor-cycle was much better than a night spent on books or diagrams. He did, however, stress that care had to be taken with tramlines and that there was a divergence of opinion as to the best horsepower, but that 1 or 2 was the minimum.

What seem to have been Bolton Corporation's first positive thoughts about the potential of motor vehicles were aired in December 1902, when the Streets Committee resolved to ask the Council 'to consider and report as to the adoption of self-propelled motor vehicles for the purposes of the department.'

Later the same month, the Electricity Sub-Committee announced that they had made arrangements for 'lectures on Motor Driving.'

The Manchester Association of Merchants and Manufacturers considered the possibility of moving heavy goods by motor haulage at their Board Meeting in January 1903. The past president of the Association advocated a motor road service between the Manchester

An early Vulcan, reputed to have been worked on at Bolton Technical School in 1899. The Hampson brothers are seated.

Ship Canal and the cotton mills of Bolton, Oldham, Royton, Stockport, Ashton and Burnley, with return journeys with finished goods. The current President, J H Butterworth, thought the idea good, but considered that the matter should be held in abeyance as he felt that 'some improvements should be done to present vehicles.'

On 18th March 1903 the Bolton Evening News 'Cycling Notes' discussed the relative merits of £50 and £35 motorcycles. The reporter had made enquiries at Madgwicks, Coopers of Howell Croft and the Palatine Company of 109 Bradshawgate and all could offer a 2hp machine for £35. The following week he was taken to task by some other suppliers of machines in the £35 range, with one of them saying that he only made £2 profit on the sale of such machines.

Cases of traffic misdemeanours received due attention in the Bolton Evening News. A report in April 1903 concerned Henry Robinson, the Bath Street cycle maker and dealer. He was riding a motor tricycle - probably a De Dion - down Knowsley Street at an alleged 10-20mph, with Mrs Robinson seated in the wicker basket chair at the front. PC Pye claimed that he was nearly knocked down and, as he stepped out of the way, Robinson smiled at him. In court, Robinson said it was impossible to reach the alleged speed as it was only a 2hp machine. In his opinion he was only doing 6mph and in any case, he dared not drive any faster owing to his wife's nervous disposition. The case was dismissed.

The dangers of motor racing on public roads was drawn to the attention of Bolton Evening News readers in May 1903. The Paris - Madrid race was stopped at Bordeaux by the French authorities on account of the number of casualties among competitors and spectators. This was the last of the epic road races between Paris and other European capitals.

In Britain, racing on public highways was expressly forbidden under the 1835 Highways Act and the Highways & Locomotives (Amendment) Act of 1878, which could be invoked to punish 'furious driving' and 'interrupting the free use of the Highway to others'. Separate provisions in law enabled road racing to be conducted in Ireland and on the Isle of Man, and on municipal promenades at seasides.

Local businessmen were by now aware that the mechanically propelled vehicle was something with a future. For heavy industrial haulage, the steam vehicle had the advantage over the petrol engine, which at this time was mainly suitable for light vehicles. Bolton's Registers of Heavy Motor Cars contain details of the early makes and their owners.

Local brewers Magee Marshall & Co registered a Thornycroft steamer, BN33, on 1st January 1904. Another Thornycroft, BN58, was acquired by John Smith, chemical manufacturer of Great Lever, and in February the engineering firm of Entwisle & Gass in Thynne Street registered BN72, a steamer of their own design and make.

These pioneering vehicle operators seem to have made quite an impression, for between January and October 1905 a further nine steamers were registered. Ormrod's Brickworks at Jacksons Quarry, Edgefold, invested in Mann steam tippers; Ashworth's New Eagley Mills registered a Yorkshire Patent, and Phillipson's of Bromley Cross Quarry a steamer made locally by the Bolton Motor Wagon Co, Turk Street, off Chorley Old Road. This firm registered three more of their own make for haulage on demand or contract.

In the 1930s the Bolton Evening News printed some articles recalling the early days in Bolton's motoring history. Mr W Forrest Bowen of 'Stonewall', Blackburn Road, wrote that he owned a 5hp Decauville, registered BN9, and a friend, Thomas Caldwell, a 4hp New Orleans, registered BN8.

They had travelled down to Cambridge in their respective cars without too much bother. As his car could only reach 24mph (legal limit 20mph), this would have been something of an epic run diagonally across England, possibly at some point crossing the Pennines or the Peak District.

Mr Bowen said that he regularly travelled to Blackpool, Preston and Southport, and that he had bought the car some three years before registering it in December 1903. He went on to claim that, 'The best run I ever had in the old BN9 was coming back from Chester in a gale. I did it in little over an hour.' This must be the motoring equivalent of the fisherman's tale of the one that got away. To cover the 40-odd miles between Chester and Bolton, via Frodsham, Preston Brook, Warrington and Leigh, his little voiturette must have been running before the gale!

An early advertisement for Edmund Holden, one of Bolton's first motor garage and omnibus proprietors

14

Writing in 1935, Thomas Brown, the 71-year-old proprietor of the Spa Garage in Bolton, recalled when he was an engineer living in the Kirkham area. His introduction to motor cars came via a paraffin-engined model owned by a Mr Birley of Milbanke House, Kirkham, who had purchased it abroad and had not been able to get it to run properly.

Mr Brown corrected the fault to Mr Birley's satisfaction and the following year he went on to build a small car for a Mr Kay of Lytham. This was powered by a two-cylinder horizontal petrol engine and had a final drive by belt. It took them from Saturday noon until Monday night to travel from Lytham to Harrogate, the main problem being tyre punctures. Tyres 'were largely in the experimental stage and not equal to a 17cwt car.'

The next car Mr Brown drove was a 12/16hp Panhard owned by Mr Thomas Magee of Lytham Hall and Lower House, Lostock. He drove from Lytham to Nice in 1902, and in order to comply with French regulations, he had to pass a driving and engineering test by two officials from the Ministry of Mines, which was the controlling authority at that time. The licence issued was more like a passport and contained personal details and a photograph. He drove the car all over the Côte d'Azur and brought it back via London, where Mr Magee attended the Coronation of Edward VII. On the way back to Lytham he was booked by the police for exceeding the 12mph speed limit in Chorley by 2mph but, 'thanks to the efforts of two Bolton solicitors,' the case never reached the courts. On 1st January 1903 the car was registered as BN50.

George Edward Cain was another of Bolton's pioneer motorists. Pre-1900 directories describe him as a tripe dealer, with premises in Deansgate and Bradshawgate, then in the early 1900s he was a 'commission agent', followed by 'turf accountant'. His office was in Silverwell Street, an area with businesses which could enhance his wealth in a discreet manner. He lived at 'Rostrevor', 44 Bromwich Street, the Haulgh, an area for the successful middle class.

His first car was a 10hp Lanchester, tiller steered, with an air cooled engine and registered BN103 in April 1904. As a result of some difference of opinion regarding the relative merits of the car and the horse, he decided to mount the Town Hall steps to prove his point. (Whether anyone had ever ridden a horse up the steps has yet to be determined.) His action brought him into contact with the Bolton police, who successfully prosecuted him for 'endangering public property.'

Mr Cain's next car was a French Richard-Brasier of 1905/6 vintage and registered BN221. Another of his cars was a 1912 Mercedes tourer, a powerful machine in its day, and not cheap. He apparently had the car brought up to date by 1914, with electric head and side lamps replacing the acetylene versions.

By 1900 Bolton's trams covered most areas, but the service had not reached Darcy Lever, owing to the state of the road and the steep drop into the valley. During negotiations for the township's inclusion into the Borough, a promise was made that some form of public transport would be provided.

In June 1902 a deputation from Darcy Lever asked the Council about progress and were told little could be done at the moment. In March 1903 the Council was asked about a motor bus and a letter from Messrs Milnes-Daimler of London regarding a six-month trial was read out. The Council decided to defer their decision until their meeting on 11th May, by which time Milnes-Daimler had sold the whole of their year's output of double-deckers.

Magees Brewery yard in the early twentieth century, as horse transport was giving way to the motor lorry

Two months later J V Madgwick offered a wagonette, which was turned down as unsuitable, but he did later arrange for the supply of the first motor-bus. This was a 2-cylinder, 12hp Stirling which arrived from Edinburgh early in November after a journey via Carlisle and Shap Fell, taking three days at 12mph. The price of £750 was high, even by Edwardian standards. Trials were fairly successful, but hampered by tyre and mechanical troubles, the bus disappeared to an unknown fate after December.

A 4-cylinder, 25hp version was ordered from Stirlings in February 1904 and it arrived in early August. The Bolton Journal gave an account of its testing, with members of the Tramway Committee, the Borough Engineer, Borough Electrical Engineer, Mr Madgwick and two reporters from the paper on board. The vehicle cost £850, had a 25hp engine, a 9-gallon fuel tank (considered enough for 100 miles) and a three-speed gearbox with speeds of 4, 8 and 11mph.

The bus began running in early September from Mealhouse Lane to the Bowling Green Hotel in Brownlow Fold. On return, it went to Darcy Lever Wesleyan Chapel for a fare of one penny. However, persistent tyre and mechanical troubles meant that it ran on only 12 out of 28 days and it was returned to the makers in October. News of this even reached the editor of The

Autocar magazine, and the Bolton Evening News of 22nd October reported that the magazine suggested mismanagement, because other models had 'succeeded elsewhere, so why not Bolton?' The editor advised the Corporation to try again and take some expert advice, because the bus was habitually overloaded and broke down through sheer lack of attention. The magazine also said that Bolton Corporation 'holds this example up as a warning to other municipalities.'

Next, the Council agreed to provide Darcy Lever with a horse-bus, on hire from Edmund Holden. This ran from the Swan Hotel to Darcy Lever via Castle Street and Radcliffe Road until July 1907. More buses were tested in that year, with varying degrees of success. January saw a 40/50hp Ryknield, February a Darracq-Serpollet steamer, June a British Thomson-Houston petrol-electric model. The Council settled on the Darracq-Serpollet, bought it for £1,025 and put it into service in July. The horse-bus had never made a profit and the weekly loss averaged £2.10s; the new bus made £1 a week profit during the first three months' service.

After a somewhat troublesome career, the steamer was replaced by a Straker-Squire and then a Commer, which ran on the route until the laying of tramlines into Darcy Lever and the opening of the

Percy Langton Birley, one of Lancashire's first motorists and an early customer of Thomas Brown, who later ran the Spa Garage in Bolton

line in May 1910. The Commer seems to have been kept in some sort of service until at least 1912 and it appears that other buses were in operation, since in March the Tramways Committee resolved that 'the present tyres and wheels of buses be returned to makers and that their tender for a supply of new tyres be accepted.' The Bolton bus service as we know it today started in December 1923 with a bus borrowed from Leyland Motors, followed in March 1924 by five bought from them.

The Motor Car Act of 1904 set a speed limit of 20mph, but it rested with local authorities to apply to the Government for permission to impose limits in towns, cities and country districts. The fact that Bolton decided on the 20mph limit in 1904 is clear from a Bolton Evening News report of 6th January 1905, when Col George Kemp, MP for Heywood, appealed against a £5 fine and licence endorsement for speeding past the Sportsmans Arms at Montserrat. He was heading towards Bolton in an 11hp Panhard at an alleged rate of between 20 and 30mph, and the car appeared to be out of control. As no comment was made, presumably his appeal failed.

Fixed roadside signals to advise motorists of hazards or speed restrictions were another aspect of the new Act. A conference of county council and municipal corporations

George Edward Cain driving his 1912 Mercedes. The original lamps were probably acetylene, but it was converted to electric lighting in 1914

in January 1904 agreed the following:

1. For a 10mph (or lower) limit, a white ring, 18 inches in diameter, with a plate below giving the limit in figures.

2. For prohibition, a solid red disc, 18 inches in diameter.

3. For caution (dangerous corners, crossroads, etc) a hollow red equilateral triangle with 18-inch sides.

4. All other notices under the Act to be on diamond-shaped boards on the nearside of the road facing the driver and located approximately 50 yards from the particular hazardous spot and not less than 8 feet from the ground.

It is interesting to note that at the time there were no road signs indicating derestriction following a speed limit notice.

Thomas Hampson of Wigan was an early motor pioneer who came to Bolton in 1892 as a 'Manual Instructor' in wood and metal at the Bolton Technical Institute.

Whilst there, he and his brother Joseph built a small petrol engined car with a belt drive transmission. One of the problems with this system was the fact that the belt stretched and slipped due to weather conditions. To rectify this, Thomas designed and patented a belt tensioning device. His address on the patent was 385 Halliwell Road, Bolton.

Early in 1900 the brothers opened a small works making motor cars in Southport. In 1903 the firm was named the Vulcan Motor Manufacturing & Engineering Co and a few years later serious motor vehicle manufacturing began at a new works at Crossens.

The firm's fortunes declined after the 1914-18 war. Production of cars ceased in 1928 and commercial vehicles in 1930, when the business was sold. With regard to the car made at Bolton Technical College, it was converted to mechanical transmission at Harold Ainscough

Heaton's garage in Davenport Street for an unknown customer and later disappeared into a local scrapyard.

Of Bolton's first garages, the one founded by J V Madgwick seems to have been the most progressive. It was named the Bolton Motor Company and its aims were set out in a Bolton Evening News advertisement of 13th January 1904. The showrooms were at 121-123 St Georges Road, with repair and garage premises in Back Bark Street. 'The operation consists of repairs of motor vehicles, cars, bicycles and lorries, while in the showroom and at the works in Back Bark Street will be displayed specimens of the 10hp Lanchester, the 45hp racing Wolseley capable of running a mile a minute, and other machines for which the Company has been appointed agents... A staff of employees has been brought from Birmingham, the home of the Lanchester, a handsome machine, elegantly equipped, and repair jobs are already in hand.'

The original subscribers to the company were:

Frank Eckersley of 'Penrhos Lodge', Sale, Cheshire. Cotton spinner. (Director)

Richard Slater of 9 Westwood Road, Bolton. Bleacher. (Director)

James Veoux Madgwick of 79 Knowsley Street. Motor and cycle agent. (Director)

Fred Horrocks Ward of 30 Wyresdale Road, Bolton. Cotton waste dealer.

William Kevan of 12 Acresfield, Bolton. Chartered accountant.

Henry Percival Hollindrake of 6 Queensgate, Bolton. India rubber and steam packing manufacturer. Associated with John Miles: works, Shiffnall Street, Bolton.

William Herbert Tate of 8 Oxford Street, Bolton. Saddler.

The new company was determined to make an impression and in his column of 10th March 1904, now headed 'Cycle and Motor Notes', Rambler wrote that it was the only Bolton firm with a stand at the Manchester Motor Show in St James's Hall. The stand was in the middle of the hall with a sectioned Wolseley engine driven by an electric motor. According to Rambler, this engine was 'the hit of the show' and he added that the company was showing Wolseley, Lanchester and other makes and had two available for demonstration runs in the city. The Bolton Motor Company remained at St Georges Road until 1909, when they moved to Jubilee Buildings, Marsden Road.

Mr Cain and a companion in his Richard-Brasier. Note the absence of a windscreen. The folding hood would have been secured to some form of brackets at the front and would have given some protection to the driver from an overhanging peak. The gear and handbrake levers restrict the driver's side entrance, and the serpentine bulb horn attached to the front wing was a fashionable fitting of the day. The headlamps appear to be acetylene and the side lamps gas-powered

The design of early motor cars, and the varied methods by which moving parts of the engine and transmission were lubricated, together with non-existent or indifferent sealing methods, resulted in roads being liberally sprinkled with oil or grease droppings. In April 1904 Rambler complained about 'dirty oil on our highways' and its adverse effect on cycle tyres. He returned to the topic in May, saying tramcars were 'a major culprit' and heavy lorries 'do a lot'. He suggested that some form of receptacle on the axles, etc, 'might help a lot.'

Rambler did try to be wide-ranging in his reporting of the Bolton motoring scene and in September 1904 he described a local motorcyclist's day trip to North Wales via Conway, Llanrwst, Betws-y-Coed and Llangollen, covering 201 miles in 22 hours. The remarkable thing about this run was that it was done on a 2hp machine towing a two-man tandem. He spent 12 hours in the saddle and 2 looking for petrol. The trip cost 2/4d in fuel and just to prove that it was not a one-off, he repeated the journey the next weekend, reducing the time by 2 hours.

1904 saw a variety of new and second-hand cars and motorcycles offered for sale in the Bolton Evening News. In January the Automobile & Steam Wagon Works of All Saints Street offered an unnamed two-seater 5hp car with a two-speed belt drive, an Argyle 6hp six-seater, 'splendid hill climber,' and a Thornycroft steam wagon. In March, motorcycles offered for sale from 22 Luton Street, Burnden, included a 3hp 'nearly new' Rex for £35, a 2hp Barter with side-carriage for £27 and a 1hp Minerva for £15.

In June J V Madgwick offered two motorcycles at reduced prices: a Raleigh with a list price of £55 could be had for £35 and a Clyde with 'magneto ignition, girder forks, Brookes saddle, all best fittings' listed at £54.10s, was £37.10s, including licence, registration and number plates. On 11th July Mr Openshaw of 117 Newport Street advertised his 1904 Rex motorcycle 'as he was buying a car'. Later in the

Bolton Corporation's second Stirling petrol bus, photographed in 1904. Note the narrow section, solid rubber tyres, ideal for fouling in tramlines

month a Mr Isherwood of 242 Darwen Road, Bromley Cross, offered his new Darracq 9hp four-seater with 'splendid lamps' and two extra fuel tanks for £210. A box number advertised a 6hp De Dion, bought for '£255 last July' which would 'carry four top speed Chorley New Road' for £130.

In August the All Saints Automobile Works offered 'A handsome small car' in the shape of a 6hp Vulcan. In November the Cycle and Motor Works, Rose Hill, offered a 3hp Rex motorcycle for £23 and a four-seater Benz 'on pneumatic tyres' for £27. On 12th December the Central Motor Works, 82 Town Hall Square (under the management of Alfred Kirk; owned jointly by Thomas Fitton and James Henry Green and founded about 1904) announced that now was the 'best time to have your car or motor-cycle overhauled.' They also offered a 6hp MMC car 'cheap for quick sale, will climb any hill' for 55 guineas, and a De Dion tricar for 14 guineas.

During 1905 the Carlton Motor Co of 17 Bridgeman Place, owned by Isaiah Dootson and his partner Henry Wilkinson, advertised as the sole agent for Talbot cars. Two such models were offered in March, a 14hp for £300 and an 11hp for £275.

There was also a '6hp genuine De Dion, many extras, beautiful car, £170.' In May Dootson had a 'Superior Talbot for hire with experienced driver,' and offered to convey four passengers on day trips to Blackpool, Southport, Lancaster, Morecambe, Chester and Knutsford for £3.3s. He was also prepared to go to Windermere or Colwyn Bay for an extra £1.1s.

Isaiah Dootson was also one of Bolton's early taxi proprietors. On 15th July 1904 he was the registered owner of BN130, a 10hp Decauville, Tonneau model, and licensed for 'Public as well as Trade and Private use.' His address at that time was 'Spring Lawn', Heaton. He also advertised repairs and driving instruction for the buyers of his cars.

In March 1905 the Bolton Evening News reported that an application for a 10mph limit within the borough's boundaries had been rejected by the Local Government Board. Three days later the paper reported that Mr Cawley, MP, intended to speak in Parliament on the subject of speed limits, and to ask the President of the Local Government Board if he would look more favourably on speed applications in view of the many motor accidents.

On 17th May Rambler wrote about 'Motor Fright', citing a recent case of two lady cyclists on Chorley New Road who wobbled into each other as a car passed, then had an 'upset'. The car did not stop and Rambler observed that some motorists possess 'a ghoulish delight in driving up to cyclists and then blowing the horn.' He considered that a 'timely tootle' would be best for all concerned. 'Even a man with iron nerves feels none too sure when a brute comes hurtling by him at 30-to-the-hour.'

On 1st June 1905 the Bolton Evening News reported a Parliamentary debate in which Mr Cathcart Wason said, 'to a large extent the users and drivers of motor-cars had abused their privileges.' Mr Soames agreed: 'On many country roads it seemed that Hell had been let loose. As a class, motorists could not be trusted to act like gentlemen. Fines were no deterrent, and the magistrates should have the power to imprison anyone for reckless driving on the first conviction.'

On 10th July 1905 the Bolton Evening News reported the case of Mr Edward Bertram of Appleton Wood, Egerton, described as a gentleman, who was fined £2.10s

and costs at Keswick for riding his motorcycle in excess of 30mph. When told by a policeman of his speed, he retorted, 'Oh, you fibber.'

Determining whether or not a motorist was exceeding a speed limit depended on two policemen operating what became known as a speed trap. They would stand on a stretch of road, separated by a predetermined distance and in view of each other. At the moment a suspect car passed him, Policeman A would drop a white handkerchief. On seeing it drop, Policeman B started a stop-watch, which he would stop when the car passed him. The elapsed time and the vehicle registration would form the main evidence to support a charge of exceeding the speed limit.

Bolton motorists continued to exceed speed limits and their court appearances were duly reported in the paper. In August William Rostron Pickup, described as a gentleman of Holme Lea, Lostock, was fined £7 at Lancaster for driving his car at 30mph in Warton. In his defence he said he was only going at 14mph and that he 'frequently gave up his time to educate horses to the motor-car.' In December 1905, lack

of proper evidence resulted in dismissal of the case against Fred Mason, chauffeur to Mr Marsden of 'Lymefield', Chorley New Road. PC Kindred told Bolton Borough Court that the speed was not less than 20mph and a witness was of the opinion that the car 'was going at a rate of a mile-a-minute' and 'going to Kingdom Come.' The defendant denied this and said he had 'shut off the engine and was coming down the hill by gravitation' at not more than 15mph.

Mechanical failure of heavy lorries descending gradients was an ever-present danger, at a time when braking systems were somewhat rudimentary. In October 1905 there was a report of an accident on Belmont Road, near Sweetloves reservoir.

A Yorkshire Patent steam lorry belonging to the Lancashire Explosives Co of Manchester was on its way to the Withnell Powder Works near Abbey Village when the driver had some trouble with the steam water injector. His load was transferred to another lorry and as he started going back towards Manchester, the lorry ran away. He was unable to engage reverse gear,

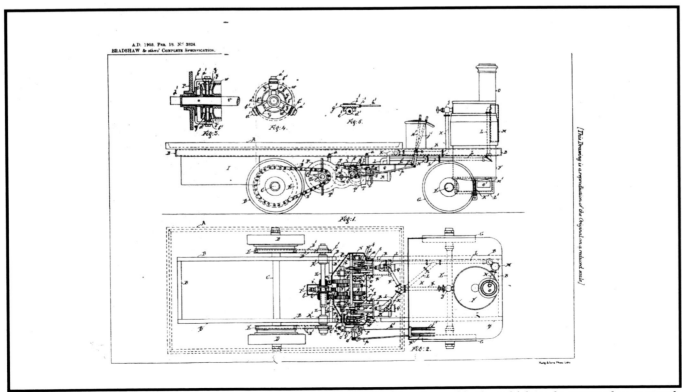

Bradshaw's steam lorry, made in Bolton. This model had a patent gearbox to enable the vehicle to be reversed as a petrol-engined vehicle, instead of having to stop the engine and manipulate the valve gear eccentrics.

the brakes failed and the lorry mounted the pavement, killing Robert Atkinson, a Corporation tram conductor of Pleasant Street, Bolton. His brother, PC Harry Atkinson of Silverdale Road, was injured.

At the inquest, Samuel Bradshaw of the Bolton Motor Wagon Company gave his expert opinion on the condition of the vehicle. He said the fault lay in the way certain cog wheels were attached to their shafts, and the brake blocks, which were timber lined with leather, were not powerful enough to stop the vehicle on an incline. The coroner returned a verdict of 'accidental death'.

Dust created by motor cars outside towns and cities, where most road surfaces were simply crushed stone, started a market for all-enveloping clothing and a Bolton pioneer in this respect appears to have been the outfitter Richard Whitehead.

In October 1905 he advertised 'Motor coats for Gentlemen. Serviceable dark grey cloth, lined throughout with fine quality Musquash Skins, all backs; large Collar of Real Beaver. 12gns.'

By about 1907 closed cars had become fairly commonplace so that motorists could dress in a more comfortable manner. Also from that time, main roads outside towns were covered with tarmacadam or laid with stone setts.

With regard to motor vehicles and repairs, the Autoworks of All Saints Street advertised in August 1905: 'Motor tyres and air tubes vulcanised thoroughly and promptly... Cars stored, cleaned and repaired, accumulators charged, petrol, oils, fittings and parts...'

In November 1905 one of Bolton's early motor traders ceased business. This was Charles Dolden's Rose Hill Garage, opposite what was the Raikes Lane Stadium.

The contents of his garage were advertised for sale by auction and included a 4½hp Benz car, Progress, Werner, Ariel and Singer motorcycles and forty ladies' and gents' second-hand cycles.

The Bolton Motoring Scene 1906-1914

During this period the motor vehicle developed into a quite reliable means of transport and the petrol engine reached a state of engineering far removed from the comparatively crude and noisy examples produced at the turn of the century. In pursuit of increased power, engine designers increased the capacity of the engine cylinders, producing monster machines in chassis unable to cope with them, and with braking systems which were hardly able to deal with the speeds and roads encountered.

Many of these engines were of continental origin, such as the Italian Isotta-Fraschini, a 6-cylinder, 11,939cc car for 1908. In Germany, Daimler, under the name of Mercedes, produced a 6-cylinder, 10,178cc model in 1907. Fiat built a succession of 4-cylinder engines with up to 10,082cc capacity and 6-cylinder models until 1914, and Peugeot built similar engines until 1908.

Then came improvements under such engineers as William Royce, Ernest Henry and Ettore Bugatti and by 1914 the monster engines had been outclassed by designs of reduced capacity coupled with enhanced performance. These paved the way for the aircraft engines of the 1914-18 war, which, in many cases, were masterpieces of engineering and design.

Motor Racing at Rivington

Between 1906 and 1912 Bolton motorists had the opportunity to witness the performance of a variety of cars and motorcycles in the hands of some notable drivers of the day on the private roads of W H Lever (later Lord Leverhulme).

The first of these hill-climb races took place on 25th July 1906 and was limited to members of the West Lancashire Automobile Club. The cars were divided into ten classes, depending on their list prices, ranging from £200 to 'exceeding £1,000'; from Belsize and Rover cars up to 35hp Daimler, 40hp Napier, 60hp Mercedes and 70hp Darracq. 37 cars were entered and there were 27 starters. They were weighed in Horwich in the morning and then, after a suitable lunch interval, made their way to Rivington. The venue was the road directly behind the Rivington and Blackrod Grammar School. At the end of the day medals and cups were awarded and a special prize was given to the Anglo-American Oil Co.

The Club met again in July 1907 and out of 60 entries, 45 turned up. The Autocar magazine noted the average gradient was 1 in 10; the critical portion was 1km in length, with a good surface, and 'altogether it was a delightful and busy scene and a glorious day.' The cars had

Here, in July 1907, a Napier tourer takes part in a hill climb at Rivington. The driver was Selwyn Francis Edge, who held the main agency for Napier cars in London

been weighed the previous night and the drivers were reminded that they must 'avoid any doping with oxygen and other adventitious aid.' They would be disqualified for using any other fuel than petrol.

The names of the cars show that a sizeable number were from the continent: Minerva (Belgium), Darracq (France), La Buire (France), Metallurgique (Belgium), Horch (Germany), Bleriot (France) and Sizaire-Naudin (France). Some makes exist today in one form or another, or have recently disappeared: Wolseley, Talbot, Humber and Daimler.

Some were of local manufacture. Three Belsize models (6, 20 and 30hp) were made in Clayton, Manchester, by Marchall & Co, founded in 1896 to make a Benz pattern car based on the French Hurtu. The firm survived as a maker until 1925. A 30/40hp Critchley-Norris was made at Crossleys of Gorton and was chain driven, with an open body based on the Mercedes. A 10hp New Eagle was made at Broadheath by Ralph Jackson, who progressed from cycle making to founding the Century Engineering & Motor Co to make three and four-wheelers. The company was wound up in 1907 but

Jackson continued as the owner of the St Georges Motor Co, Manchester. There were two Bell cars from Ravensthorpe, Yorkshire; after the 1914-18 war these were made by the Co-op Wholesale Society in Upper Chorlton Road, Manchester.

Among the drivers was H Hollindrake in his 35hp La Buire; his name still survives in the Stockport motor trade. A Mrs E A Riley (believed to have been connected with E J Riley, billiard table maker of Accrington) drove a 20hp Belsize and came third in a field of 12 with a time of 1 minute 39 seconds to mount the hill. Aristocracy was represented by the Earl of Shrewsbury and Talbot on a 12/16hp Clement-Talbot, and Viscount Ingestre on a similar mount in the 15/20hp class.

In June 1909, the 26 cars entered for the hill climb were divided into horsepower classes as determined by the Treasury formula created for taxation under the 1909 Finance Act. The classes ranged from a maximum 'greater than 35hp' down to 'not greater than 12hp.' In the former class was a Manchester engineer, Mr Higginson, with his 80hp La Buire tourer. It was, according to the Autocar, 'the monster of the show'.

An interesting feature of these Rivington races was that entrants had to carry a full complement of passengers, the ladies suitably hatted and veiled, as can be seen in the contemporary photographs.

In October 1912 the venue was used by the Liverpool Autocycle Club. The variety of mounts in the field of about 200 is an indication of the extent of the motorcycle's popularity: Zenith, Rudge, Ivy, Douglas, Matchless, Triumph, Singer, Humber and Dot, to name a few. One entrant, Mr Longden, carried his pet dog in the sidecar of his 8hp Dot. This machine had been made in Hulme, Manchester, since 1903 by Henry Reed, the name having reputedly been derived from 'Devoid Of Trouble'.

As far as official racing is concerned, this seems to have been the last time such an event was held at Rivington. Over the years, the Bolton Motorcycle Club occasionally made the 'run', and from time to time Territorial Army dispatch riders mounted the hill to prove their competence over all types of terrain.

The impressive performance of Napier cars at the Rivington Hill Climb meetings brought four of the more powerful models to Bolton.

Two privately owned cars inside Gordon's garage before 1914. The 30hp Daimler landaulette BN501 was first registered on 24th June 1909 by Edward Deakin of Egerton Hall. The 10hp Delage two-seater BN807 was registered on 25th September 1912 by J A Barber-Lomax of Bolton. On the running board is an acetylene gas generator for headlamps, and above it an elegant oil side lamp

The prices ranged from £250 for the small, 10hp model to £1,500 for a 90hp model. A comparable 45hp Mercedes cost £825 without a body. Four Bolton businessmen purchased Napier cars:

Joseph Sharman, a brewer, of 'The Hollies', a 40hp Tonnau-bodied tourer, registered BN381 on 22nd July 1907;

T H Thwaites, a bleacher, of 'Watermillock', a similar model of 40hp, registered BN404 on 9th October 1907;

Norman Fletcher, a businessman of 'The Hollins', a 30hp double Phaeton, registered BN453 on 1st July 1908;

Alfred Glaister of Breightmet Hall, a 40hp Landaulette, registered BN472 on 12th December 1908.

By 1908 it was apparent that some form of driver instruction would benefit all concerned. In the September, Bolton Council received a letter from the Local Government Board regarding 'the dangers and annoyance caused by driving motor cars,' and recommended that a copy of Section 1 of the Motor Car Act of 1903/4 be given to each person obtaining a driver's licence. This section was concerned with general conduct, speed limits and consideration for other road users.

A few firms offered driving tuition as part of the sale of a car, but most drivers were taught either by relatives or friends, or simply learned by trial and error on their own. (The official driving test did not appear until 1935.) Advertising in 1936, the Surefleet Motor School of Derby Street claimed to have 30 years' experience, which suggests that members of the firm were involved in tuition in 1906. About three years after this, the Bolton School of Motoring was in operation under Messrs Entwistle & Walker - later garage proprietors in Derby Street.

The increase in traffic volume and its attendant hazards gradually became the subject of deliberation in the Bolton Council Chamber. On 23rd June 1909 the Watch Committee agreed to place signs on Wigan Road near to Deane Schools (Hulton Lane/Deane Church Lane) to warn motorists of possible delays.

Traffic in the town centre received some attention, with agreement to place a constable on point duty at the junction of Bridge Street and Bow Street. The Bolton Co-op was at its zenith then, and since the main warehouse had its outlet into the narrow Bow Street, congestion was no doubt particularly heavy during the morning, when horse lorries set out on their delivery runs.

In August 1909 the Watch Committee decided to take a census of motor traffic at three points in the borough over the period of a week. The results were:

1. Green Lane/Manchester Road: 786 motor cars, 39 covered motor vans, 6 motor omnibuses, 241 rubber tyred motor lorries, 5 rubber tyred trailers, 250 steel tyred motor lorries, 178 steel tyred trailers, 2 traction engines with 6 trailers.

2. Bridge Street/Bow Street: 400 motor cars, 14 covered motor vans, 2 motor omnibuses, 112 rubber tyred motor lorries, 55 steel tyred motor lorries, 28 steel tyred trailers.

3. Belmont Road/Blackburn Road: 586 motor cars, 7 covered motor vans, 107 rubber tyred motor lorries, 305 steel tyred motor lorries, 84 steel tyred trailers.

In addition to the motor vehicles, there would have been a considerable number of horse-drawn lorries, vans and cabs; motorcycles and pedal cycles. Also, Corporation trams travelled along most of the roads in and around the town, contributing to the traffic problems, particularly in the Bow Street area.

Local businesses also played their part, continuing to increase their fleets of lorries into the post-war years.

The Lancashire & Yorkshire Railway Co employed a road carting contractor in the shape of Sir Joseph Nall & Co, whose black Clydesdale draught horses were once a familiar sight on the streets of Bolton. Their first vehicle registered in Bolton was an Aveling-Porter traction engine in 1906. Four years later they registered a Leyland steam lorry.

The firm was based in Manchester, so they would no doubt have had other vehicles of their embryo fleet spread over a number of depots.

Between November 1919 and January 1920 eight Hallford petrol lorries were registered as new and given BN numbers.

Another way in which Bolton Corporation Tramways Department filled the roads. This Commer tower wagon was registered BN456 in July 1909

Brewers Magee Marshall, pioneers of Bolton's commercial transport scene, acquired four new petrol lorries in 1907. The following year the firm bought a La Coste lorry and had a charabanc body made so that it became a dual-purpose vehicle. So Magees seemingly became Bolton's first charabanc operator, perhaps offering day trips for their public house customers. Between November 1919 and August 1920 the firm registered ten more lorries, made by Karrier Motors of Huddersfield.

The old established wholesale provision merchant, Steele of Victoria Square, experimented with a Pagefield lorry (made in Wigan) in 1912 and, seemingly satisfied, purchased three more between 1916 and 1920. One was a petrol-engined Leyland, another a Straker-Squire (in reality a German Bussing, built under licence in Bristol) and the third a Burford, named after a firm of that name but in fact a Fremont-Mais imported from Ohio, USA.

Between March 1912 and December 1915 George Bertram Porteous ran some form of haulage business from 86 Deansgate. During that period he registered four new Sentinel steamers (BN861, BN1237, BN1344 and BN1928) and a 30hp Alldays petrol lorry (BN2111). What happened to this firm is unknown, as the name does not appear in the 1922 directory.

The first mill owner to register motor lorries in Bolton was John Ainscow of Bee Hive Mill, Lostock. Two unnamed vehicles, BN403 and BN455, were registered in October 1907 and July 1908. The lorries appear to have been supplied by a London agency, the Motor Emporium. A 35hp Vulcan was registered in August 1908 and a Seldon in January 1916.

Bolton Textile Mill, Moses Gate, registered a 25hp Star in October 1915, followed by two 45hp AEC lorries (BN3328 and BN3334) in November 1919. Between then and December 1920, twenty-one textile firms registered 26 lorries: 6 Star, 2 Alldays, 4 Leyland, 1 Maudsley, 2 Garner, 1 Guy, 1 GMC, 2 Albion, 1

Commer, 1 Straker-Squire, 1 Lacre, 1 Daimler, 1 Ryke, 1 Karrier and 1 Thornycroft.

Over a period of about three years from 1911 a recession in the manufacturing districts led to disputes in the textile and attendant engineering trades. One of the Bolton firms affected was Musgrave's, textile and general engineers of Kay Street.

Two employees, the brothers Percy and Harold Southern, decided on a change of career and to make their future in the town's motor trade. With some financial assistance, they acquired a brand new 14/16hp Belsize with a Landaulette body, which was registered on 23rd March 1911 as BN659, and became pioneers in the emerging taxi business. Two more vehicles, BN686 and BN770, were purchased in October 1911. The brothers had a small garage in Crumpsall Street and an office at 343 Blackburn Road, which was staffed by their sister, Miss Bertha Southern.

In February 1914 the Streets Committee approved Percy Southern's plan for a new garage on Blackburn Road and the Watch Committee agreed to extend his original (November 1911) petrol storage licence for 100 gallons to one for 350 gallons in 2 gallon tins. The petrol store was 'to be erected at the rear of the new garage opposite the coal siding in Blackburn Road.' The

firm evolved into Southern Brothers Ltd, Austin main agents of Bolton, and remained in the town until 1982.

When the Austin Motor Co celebrated its Golden Jubilee in 1955, Southern Brothers Ltd advertised in the commemorative issue of The Autocar, stating, 'We are justifiably proud that in 1911 our founders were first privileged to secure the Austin Agency in the area.'

How the brothers managed to secure an agency at such an early date is something of a mystery. Older members of the firm were of the opinion that Musgrave's had done machine work for Herbert Austin, so the Southerns would already have known him. David Scott-Moncreiff, in his 1955 book on veteran and Edwardian cars, states that the Austin Motor Co had some involvement with textile machine making before 1914, and this could explain the connection with Musgraves.

The first motor taxi proprietors in Bolton were probably Messrs Taylor & Temperley of Bradford Buildings, Mawdsley Street, who were granted permission for a 'motor-car Hackney Carriage' by the Watch Committee on 30th August 1905. Another pioneer was the Bolton Mutual Garage, Byng Street, Bradshawgate, granted a motor hackney licence for two passengers on 8th April 1908.

An early car belonging to Southern Brothers

On 28th January 1910 the Bolton Journal announced that the Watch Committee had approved five sites from which taxis could operate - Churchgate; Trinity Street and Great Moor Street Railway Stations; the north side of Victoria Square and the Crofters Hotel at the junction of Chorley Old and New Roads. At the Watch Committee meeting on 27th September 1911, a letter from Joseph Barrett, Percy Southern and William Hall, 'representing the Motor-Cab Proprietors in Bolton,' was read out. They asked for permission for their taxis to stand at the approach to Trinity Street Station, which was in effect a request to be able to ply for hire. The application was refused, and so was their request for a cab shelter on Victoria Square.

By 1914 motor traction of one sort or another was becoming essential in the conduct of the town's affairs. The unfortunate episode of the Darcy Lever bus no doubt coloured opinion, but councillors could not ignore the many advantages the petrol engine had over the horse and cart.

A motor tower wagon for servicing overhead tram wires was discussed in May 1903, but it was not until January 1907 that the Tramways Committee noted that £735 had been paid to Milnes-Daimler for a tower wagon chassis. The vehicle, with a tower probably taken from a horse-drawn lorry, was registered as BN335 in January 1907. The licence was transferred to a 45hp tower wagon in June 1919.

The next department to become motorised appears to have been the Waterworks. In April 1910 Vulcan Motors of Southport were paid £452.12s for a car for the Engineer. He was also provided with a 'Motor Coat and Cap' for £2.17.8d.

In August 1909 a sub-committee was appointed to look into the provision of a motor-ambulance for the Fire Brigade. (There was no separate Ambulance service at this time.) Six months later it was decided not to have one, then on 15th January 1913 it was finally resolved that a motor-ambulance would be an asset. The same

meeting also agreed that motor traction should be adopted by the Fire Brigade per se. The Austin Motor Co won the supply contract for the vehicle, BN1235, with 'a special ambulance Brougham body' in dark imperial green with a cream stripe. It went into service in May 1913. To ensure some priority on the roads in an emergency, the Fire Brigade Superintendent was asked to make enquiries 'for a suitable signal horn.'

What appears to have been the first motorised ambulance for public service in Bolton was registered BN1140 on 10th March 1913. It was a 15/20hp vehicle, possibly an Austin, for the Bolton Union Guardians, and was 'in natural colours, and the framework chocolate.'

The question of a motorised fire appliance was discussed in 1903 and again in 1910, after the Fire Brigade Sub-Committee had been to Bury to see a Merryweather fire engine tested, but it was not until the appointment of Herbert Bentley as Bolton's Fire Chief that the matter was resolved.

With the aid of a £1,000 loan from the Local Government Board, a 45hp, 6-cylinder Leyland/Merryweather fire engine was acquired in 1913. It weighed six tons and had an estimated top speed of 50mph. There were twin rear wheels and single fronts, with solid rubber

tyres. The Rees Roturbo pump could produce 600 gallons per minute at 120lbs per square inch pressure, with a 10-foot lift of water. Maximum pressure was 200lbs psi in a lift of 27 feet and the water jet could reach 200 feet. The engine was equipped with 180 feet of hose and a Merryweather demountable escape ladder on a wheeled chassis.

The extent of municipal interest in the motor vehicle can perhaps be judged by an entry in the Waterworks Committee minutes for 2nd December 1914. The Town Clerk had obtained tenders for a minimum supply of 5,000 gallons of petrol to be delivered to various depots over the next 12 months. It was decided that no advantage could be gained by bulk storage.

The heavy wear and tear of road surfaces caused by the phenomenal growth in the number of motor vehicles reached a point where local authorities were unable to cope with maintenance and repair costs. They were also concerned that much of the damage was caused by passing traffic over which they had no control in the form of registration fees under the 1903 Act.

The scene was set for a major change in road funding and after due deliberation the Government decided that monies raised from motor taxation should go into the Road Fund, from which local

Vulcan Motors also provided this 20hp charabanc for John H Bromilow, seen here as the driver. Judging by the varied headgear, the party, photographed outside the Victoria Hotel in 1914, were on a holiday trip

authorities would be paid towards road maintenance in their jurisdictions; inter-town main roads would be Government responsibility. Under the 1909 Road Improvement Funds Act, a motor vehicle was taxed according to the RAC Formula, which was used to calculate the theoretical horsepower of the engine based on piston area. A petrol tax of 3d per gallon also contributed to the Road Fund.

The Chancellor of the Exchequer, David Lloyd George, stated that, 'not a penny of the Fund will be touched by the Chancellor of the Exchequer for other purposes... the money will be spent on the roads of the country.' This soon changed. In 1915, when petrol tax was raised to 6d a gallon, the extra revenue was extracted from the Road Fund and used for the general purposes of the war.

The Road Fund was raided by successive Chancellors over the years, then in 1936 Neville Chamberlain allowed the Treasury to have the full £31.5 million annual motor and fuel taxes. According to The Motor magazine, the Treasury 'could dole out what it liked for the roads from year to year.'

The closing years of the reign of Edward VII and the early ones of George V saw further growth in the motor trade in Bolton to accommodate the expanding number of private and commercial vehicle owners.

A 1909 advertisement for the Bolton Mutual Garage of Byng Street, near the corner of Bradshawgate and Trinity Street, seemed to be aimed at the reasonably well off. They were agents for Daimlers with engines of 3.3 to 10.4 litres capacity (needed for the ponderous coach-built bodies of the time); the Italian SCAT (Societa Ceirano Automobili Torino), which had links with Newton & Bennett, pioneer motor traders in Manchester; FIAT (Fabrica Italiana Automobili Torino), with large capacity engines and coachwork designed to be chauffeur driven, and Metallurgique, the large-scale Belgian sports and touring car. The garage advertised that 'other high-

class cars could be obtained without difficulty' and for customers lower down the social scale, they were sole agents for the 'famous Vulcan'.

Maurice Edwards, founder of Edbro Ltd, was the manager of the Bolton Mutual Garage in 1906 and in that year he and his brothers, William and Charles, obtained a patent for an improved carburettor design.

Four years later they patented a two-stroke horizontal piston air-cooled engine 'particularly suitable for aeroplanes.' An association with the aircraft maker A V Roe of Manchester created a market for these engines, which were sold as 'Avro' make.

In 1911 the small engineering firm of H W Cowley of Bella Street, Daubhill, were advertised as 'makers of flight engines' and evidence seems to suggest that the Edwards carburettor was a standard fitment and that the engines were, in fact, assembled in the Bolton Mutual Garage.

A two-cylinder example of the Edwards engine has been preserved in the Brooklands Motor Museum, having arrived there from Ireland, where it once powered a Farman-type aeroplane that had been built

and flown by a Miss Lillian Bland. It was christened the Mayfly and was reputed to have been the first powered aeroplane in Ireland.

Two other traders who were to have a long association with the Bolton motor world emerged during this period. In 1908/09 Stanley Parker of Westbrook Street, Manchester Road, opened the Stanley Garage, dealing in second-hand motorcycles.

About the same time Walter Bradley established an engineering works in Central Street, Deansgate, to manufacture his patent safety device for textile machinery and a few years later he added motor engineering, which developed into the main part of the business.

Walter Bradley was born in Tonge Moor and the family home was his father's butcher's shop at 2/4 Thicketford Road. He studied engineering at Bolton Technical School and between the ages of 19 and 24 worked as an engineer in Europe.

After returning to Bolton, in June 1907 he obtained a patent for a locking device which prevented the opening of an access panel on a carding engine whilst the machinery was in motion. An article in the

William Edwards' garage in Dawes Street, where his son Maurice learnt his trade

Bolton Civic Week booklet (1929) claimed that over 60,000 of these had been sold all over the world, and 'thousands had been made and fitted on a royalty basis by all the leading textile engineers.'

Mr Bradley became a councillor, then Chairman of the Corporation Transport Committee and Mayor in 1945 and 1953. His garage survived well into the post-1939/45 war period and his showroom is now a shop on Deansgate.

In 1911 Stanley and Arthur Manchester of the West End Garage, off St Georges Road, were given permission to hold 200 gallons of petrol for their taxi business. In March they advertised they had a number of second hand cars for sale and would also supply any make of car. They had at least two vehicles, both Belsize Landaulettes, BN1633 and BN1634, registered in June 1914. The following year the garage was bought by Southern Brothers.

William Henry Legat, a manufacturing chemist, had premises in St Georges Street under the sign of the 'Cross Axes' from about 1903, when plans for an office were approved. He subsequently formed W H Legat, Son & Co, motor factors and oil and grease manufacturers and by May 1914 they were sufficiently established to take over the 100-gallon petrol storage licence for 56 Bridge Street, which had belonged to Lewis Merrall Brown. Their garage was at 108-110 Great Moor Street, and the firm was later styled Legat & Dawson Ltd.

When the Bolton Motor Company moved to the Jubilee Buildings at the corner of Marsden Road in 1909, their former works and showroom on St Georges Road was occupied by Lewis Merrall Brown. Under the imposing title the Premier Motor Engineering Co, the firm had the Briton and Peugeot cars agencies and operated through the 1914-18 war, when it began making cars to its own designs. Peugeot is still a major car manufacturer, but the Briton, made by the Star Cycle Co of Wolverhampton, did not survive beyond 1922.

The site of Morrison's supermarket in the town centre covers the site of another of Bolton's early garages. The Parkfield Garage in Dawes Street was run by William Edwards and his sons. They were an early agent for the Ford Model T, made at Trafford Park, and to some extent the garage was a foundation stone of Edbro plc, as Maurice Edwards was one of William's sons.

The creation of St Peter's Way saw the complete rebuilding of the lower portion of Bradford Street, with a bridge over the new road. This was the site of another early garage, Grosvenor Motors, which in 1913 advertised 'Ford cars immediate delivery' and 'Model Touring Cars for Hire'. By the time of its demolition, the garage was a motorcycle depot run by Syl (Sylvester) Anderton, former TT rider.

For those who did not own a motor vehicle, in 1912 Edmund Holden of Bradshawgate would take a party on a round trip of 30 miles for 2/6d each, by charabanc, wagonette or omnibus. The last two were probably horse-drawn. He also advertised a speciality of 'Taxi Weddings' and 'You ought to see our up-to-date cars.'

The growth of charabanc travel was such that an association was formed between charabanc proprietors to co-ordinate the transport of passengers to seaside resorts and local beauty spots favoured by works, Sunday Schools, public houses and clubs. The success of this encouraged John H Bromilow to purchase, in 1914, a Vulcan 18-seater coach for more intimate parties. It was shod with pneumatic tyres - the epitome of coach comfort at that time.

John Henry Bromilow of 39 Churchgate (the Boars Head public house) was an established road carrier who realised the potential of mechanically propelled wagons. Between February 1912 and June 1913 he registered three Milnes-Daimler lorries, BN824, BN948 and BN1244. They were licensed as dual purpose vehicles and had demountable bodies for load carrying and passenger work as charabancs.

A Sentinel steamer, BN2386, was registered in December 1916 for wartime munitions transport. At the end of the war, John Henry became senior partner with Maurice Edwards in the firm of Bromilow & Edwards of Bark Street, but still

Lady Lisle, one of John H Bromilow's charabancs, outside Trinity Church

retained the garage at the bottom of Bank Street (demolished in 1998 and now a car park).

Among the new names which appeared in directory lists of motor traders just before the 1914-18 war were Jimmy Green, 'the Motor Man' of 103 Derby Street; Morris & Co, motor repairers of 46/48 Folds Road, and J E Wild of Clarence Garage, Clarence Street, who informed the motoring fraternity that he was the Avon tyre stockist.

As well as the general state of road surfaces in those days, tyres were at the mercy of hazards such as horse-shoe nails, sharp flints and stones. In March 1914 it was announced that the American Vulcanising Co had moved from Stretford Road, Manchester, to 20 Silverwell Lane, Bolton, for the repair of both tyres and tubes.

The motorist who fancied a foreign car could go along to P B Grundy at the Spa Garage, Spa Road, and purchase a 10/16hp Stoewer Landaulette, made in Germany by an old established firm which survived into the Second World War era as vehicle maker to the German army. Alternatively, Samuel Gordon in Higher Bridge Street sold three types of Model T Ford - the 4-seater (£135), 2-seater (£125) and Landaulette (£180).

In January 1914 the Bolton Motor Painting Co opened for business at 158-160 Crook Street. The firm had 'Heated rooms' and heraldry painting was a speciality. The painting of motor cars in those days was a somewhat attenuated process, far removed from today's spray-gun and masking tape operation.

A top of the range repaint to achieve a deep, solid, varnished colour could take quite a time. A 1912 textbook lists 17 stages of painting, drying and rubbing down, taking a total of 48 days. An 'inferior' but satisfactory job could be done in 21 days or, with the use of enamel or lacquer, a 'bargain basement' repaint could be done in 14 days. The owner's armorial bearings or heraldic device could be painted on the relevant panels for an extra 2 guineas.

The Bolton Motoring Scene August 1914 - 1925

The Bolton motoring scene did not change much in the closing months of 1914, but the military situation was brought home with a photograph of a Red Cross motor car loaded with supplies for the Front in the local paper of 23rd October. In November there was an advertisement for, 'Excellent storage for motor-cars. Can be separated and stored in heated rooms... 209 St Georges Road.' Later in the month, the owner of a 15hp Darracq offered it for sale 'due to the war'. It was 'a sacrifice' at £60.

With an air of optimism, William Edwards & Sons of the Parkfield Garage, Dawes Street, announced that they had 'The Car for 1915' - a Bedford-Buick 15/18hp for £245. This was an American chassis, imported by General Motors of London and fitted with a British body. The garage also sold Model T Fords and there was a topical note to their advertisements: 'The tradesman who competes with a horse and cart and hand barrow against a tradesman with a Ford delivery van is like fighting a machine-gun with a bow and arrow.'

The name of another pioneer motor trader appears in the records in June 1915, when William Knowles of 469 Blackburn Road had his plans for a motor garage approved by Astley Bridge District Council. Later in the month he was permitted to store 50 gallons of petrol in 2-gallon tins.

The war situation does not seem to have given Southern Brothers much concern. With their new premises on St Georges Road, they expanded into the commercial vehicle world and in September advertised 2, 3, 4 and 5/6 ton Henry Garner chassis at prices ranging from £495 to £865. These lorries had been imported by Henry Garner Ltd of Birmingham from Gramm-Bernstein Co of Ohio, USA. The advertisement also offered another US import, a 1-ton GMC chassis (£295), and a 3-ton chassis from Belsize of Manchester (£680). In December 1915 Southerns advertised that they were official agents for Ford cars and vans, including a two-seater described as 'A Spanking Little Runabout' at £125.

Another new repairer advertised in the Bolton Journal in November

A Model T Ford van outside the Parish Church School, Churchgate, at the time of the First World War. The Bolton Evening News offices now stand on this site

1915. The Victoria Garage at 30/32 Black Bank Street, Astley Bridge, covered a wide spectrum: 'Taxi cabs, touring cars, and private landaulettes for hire, weddings &c. Motor cycles, cars, lorries, and steam wagons repaired. Motor-cars garaged and cleaned. Pupils' tuition.'

1916 saw a reduction in motor vehicle advertisements. Southerns were still in the market with a range of lorries, the Thornycroft being described as the War Office model, made to the Subsidy Specification at £759. In March, Stanley Parker moved to Bradshawgate with his stock of second-hand motorcycles and the Cotton Carrying Co of Higher Bridge Street was advertised as a 'Motor Engineer and Haulage Contractor', with offices at 48 Breightmet Street.

By this time a number of the larger garages had been prevailed upon to manufacture munitions. Firms like Southerns, Walter Bradley and Gordons were accustomed to operating machine tools in the course of repairing vehicles and were thus ideal for repetitive work on sub-assembly components, as directed by a principal contract holder such as Musgraves, Hick Hargreaves or Chatwoods.

Despite the war, the Watch Committee found time to go to Leigh to inspect an ambulance and, on return, resolved to purchase a new one for the Fire Brigade. This was supplied in September by the Bolton Motor Co and insured for £700. In October, arrangements were to be made at the Fire Station for housing a motor car, 'in the event of the Watch Committee providing one for the use of the Chief Constable.'

Before petrol rationing was introduced under the Finance (No.2) Act of 1916, the motorist was asked to exercise restraint and the use of the car for pleasure was regarded as unpatriotic. There was an additional petrol tax of 6d per gallon, and prices rose to 2/4d per gallon for private use and 2/1d for a commercial user. The patriotic motorist who took his/her car off the road rather than apply for a petrol allowance was initially penalised, as the car still had to be taxed. The Secretary of the AA took this matter up with Parliament and succeeded in getting the stricture repealed.

The Eagley Co-op butcher was one of the successful local applicants for a petrol licence. The Bolton Journal of 30th August 1918 reported that he had been exempted from military service because besides selling meat, when it was available, he also ran a 13-acre farm where he grew oats and had 8 head of cattle, a horse, 28 pigs and 70-80 hens. His work was important enough for the issue of a petrol licence for his motorcycle.

Petrol rationing resulted in motorists experimenting with alternative fuels. Initially these were of the liquid, rather than gas, variety and were based on alcohol or the coal gas byproduct, benzole. The fuels were advertised under various trade titles. In June 1916 W H Legat offered Wital Motor Fuel, 'guaranteed suitable for all motors'. Messrs Lingard of 17 Churchgate had Kempal and Grandol. Whether these were accepted by Bolton motorists has yet to be discovered.

Eventually coal gas came into use as a fuel and it was the usual practice to fit a large gasbag to the roof of the vehicle and add a simple air/gas mixing device to the carburettor.

Bolton Corporation made a public supply available from the Lum Street Gasworks at a price of 1/- for the more-or-less standard 250 cubic foot gasbag, and 1d per 25cu/ft over that volume. The Bolton Journal of 28th September 1917 reported that a Bolton motorist had been to London 'by gas' at a cost of about 19/-, which was 'less than a quarter' of the petrol cost. The average price of petrol had by then risen to 4/- per gallon.

William Edwards & Sons of Dawes Street became an authorised gas filling station and announced in the Bolton Journal of 5th October: 'Eventually you must fit a gas bag to your Motor. Ask for a quotation for complete installation.' By the end of the year they were offering 'Ford size from £23.10s complete.' There was a similar advert for the Bolton Garage, opposite the Queens Cinema, Bradshawgate, but whether anyone purchased the patent rights for an unnamed 'portable gas container for motor vehicles' is questionable, since this method did not achieve much success until the early 1930s, and then more on the continent. It required a compressor capable of producing 3,000-4,000 lbs psi to fill the vehicle bottles.

The local motor scene of 1917 reflected the general demise in private car usage. Of the other firms

A Ford Model T taxi driven by Mrs E Hooton in 1917, outside her husband William's garage in Emblem Street, off Derby Street. Their children are in a home-made go-cart. The family emigrated to the USA in the mid-1920s

which managed to keep going, the Grosvenor Motor Co offered 'The New Overland Delivery Van'; Maxfield Bros of 77 St Helens Road offered 'Express Delivery 100 miles... same day,' and Stanley Parker drew the attention of motorists to the fact that he could effect immediate delivery of 1917 models of AJS, Royal Enfield, Alldays & Onions (of Birmingham) and Harley Davidson, and that 'The above machines may be purchased from us without a Ministry of Munitions Permit.'

The early months of 1918 gave little hope of a return to pleasure motoring. Speaking of the future prospects for his works, Sir Herbert Austin said, 'It is somewhat difficult to say anything in detail as the war appears to be going on for at least another two years.' The Government had a similar timescale in mind and, under the Defence of the Realm Act, a Road Transport Board was formed with three principal objects: economy in fuel consumption, maintenance of an official system of transport, and to provide for any emergency which might occur. All power driven vehicles from 15cwt upwards would have to be registered and each owner issued with a permit so that he could be called upon to place his vehicle(s) at the Government's disposal for the carriage of goods.

When the 1918 German offensive failed, the Allied military fortunes were reversed and this grand transport scheme was shelved. It was dusted off twenty years later to meet the 1939 situation and Bolton motor users were involved in its wide-ranging powers.

The ink was barely dry on the Armistice arrangements when the Watch Committee resolved, on 27th November 1918, to recommend the provision of motor vehicles and the formation of a municipal garage to provide a service for various departments. The policy was put into action in 1919, when a motor tipper was purchased for the Cleansing Department in February, a motor lorry was bought from Gordons for £292.10s in March, and a motor tractor and plough was bought for Rhodes Farm Sewage Works in May. In July it was decided to get an estimate for a police car and a large motor car would be converted into a lorry for the Waterworks, 'the smaller car to be used by the Waterworks Engineer.' The Waterworks also acquired a £600 steam lorry from the Bolton Wagon Co.

In January 1919 Southerns advertised a range of vehicles - Austin cars; Belsize, Thornycroft and Austin lorries, and Clayton steamers - pointing out that they were the sole agents for all models. For the returning serviceman considering opening his own garage, Thomas Mitchell & Sons of Derby Street advertised: 'The Coming Peace. You will require to equip your mechanics' shop with a few good machine tools. We ask for your inquiries for lathes, drilling, planing, shaping, and other machines.'

William Edwards & Sons advised potential commercial customers that they were taking orders for Vulcan 30cwt chassis, lorries complete with all accessories for £525 and complete tipping vehicles with all accessories for £575. They also had a number of chassis ready to be fitted up as commercial vehicles to carry one ton 'from £255'. This suggests that they could have been private car based and second-hand.

The tipping lorry was a result of experiments by Maurice Edwards with the hydraulic operation of tipping gears for road vehicles. It appears that this dated back to about 1916 and his association with John H Bromilow, the transport operator of Bank Street. The assembly comprised a hydraulic ram, oil supply tank, reciprocating pump and manual operating gear. A leather-faced wheel was brought into contact with the underside of the engine flywheel by means of a hand lever, thus the tipper pump was directly under the control of the operator and, with a hand throttle arrangement, the speed of discharge could be controlled. Maurice Edwards' original patent specification in July 1919 referred to a single ram; it was modified on a

An Allchin articulated three-way steam tipper outside Bromilow and Edwards' works

provisional order of October 1919 to include a twin-ram assembly.

The principle of the hydraulic ram was well established by this time, but it took the engineering genius of Maurice Edwards to apply it in a compact manner so that tipping from lorries became an easy way of unloading sand, gravel or coal. Up to this point, tippers usually employed some form of screw and crank mechanism which was both expensive to make and slow to operate. The Maurice Edwards method opened up possibilities for various functions and one of the first was the use of a single ram as a lorry mounted crane for the Anglo-Iranian Oil Co in the 1920s.

In early 1919 John H Bromilow and Maurice Edwards purchased the former Chatwood Safe Works on Bark Street and they formed Bromilow & Edwards Ltd. The firm was allocated a trade plate number on 31st March and on 30th April motor charabanc licences BN2749 and BN2778 were allocated to 'J H Bromilow, William, Charles, Maurice and Miles Edwards trading as Bromilow and Edwards, Bark Street.' The Dawes Street garage was subsequently closed and work transferred to Bark Street.

The extent of the firm's involvement in the commercial vehicle trade can be seen from an advertisement in

December 1919: 'New char-a-bancs. These should be ordered now to ensure delivery for Easter.' They were based on 4-ton AEC 28/30 seaters, 5-ton Straker-Squire 33/35 seaters and 50 cwt (originally 2.5 ton) Star 24-seaters. The firm also advertised Buick and GMC chassis on 'Lynton resilient rear wheels' (a form of cushioned solid tyre) 'and bodies which will convert [the vehicle in]to char-a-banc, bus, or flat lorry.' These had a capacity of 15 passengers or 1 ton in merchandise.

Also in December 1919, Stanley Parker of Bradshawgate in Bolton, and also of Deansgate in Manchester, offered a number of new motorcycles besides his usual stock of second-hand Triumph, New Hudson, Sunbeam, Douglas, Norton, Matchless and Enfield models. Southern Brothers on St Georges Road offered new motor-cycles, a Clyno two-stroke at £65 and a Sun with a two-stroke Villiers engine for £59.10s. William Brimelow of 111 Manchester Road advertised 5,000 tyres available at special trade terms; the Lansdowne Motor Painting Works in Cleggs Buildings, Chorley Street (Hugh Jones & Son) advertised as 'Practical Coach Painters', and a long-forgotten garage, the Service Motor Co of Haynes Street, Daubhill, would repair all makes of car and cycle.

In November 1919, under the heading, 'Bolton's Motor Boom,' a Bolton Journal reporter commented on the traffic situation in the town and the clamour for delivery of new cars: 'This seems to point to the fact that if Bolton's motor traffic is busy to-day, next year will flood our streets with pulsating hooting-tooting motor life.' He considered that the greater part of Bolton's motor traffic at the time was of the 'heavy variety' and asked, 'Have you ever counted the number of Ford tradesmen's vans that you meet in the walk home from your office?' The situation regarding delivery dates was the same in Bolton as elsewhere and he had yet to discover anyone who had taken delivery of a new 'pleasure car'. Local agents were apparently confident that orders would be met by spring 1920, but prices were unknown at that stage.

As for the type of people who wanted 'pleasure cars,' the reporter stated that they were 'nearly all folk who were prosperous enough in pre-war days to enjoy motoring as a pleasure. I'm a little bit sceptical about those artisan folk buying cars.'

The 'artisan folk' could acquire motorcycles, which were continuing to increase in popularity, but, 'How many of Bolton's would-be riders have yard-space for garage accommodation? When we get houses with decent yards, with room for a tiny garage, and with doors that will take a cycle and side-car, facilities for properly storing an expensive machine, we shall have more riders. Here's a hint for the Corporation Housing Committee, for judging from what I hear as to the rents for the new houses, they will only be occupied by the genuine middle-class.' He was referring to Bolton's first municipal housing development; the first house, at Platt Hill, Deane, was completed in 1920.

During a prolonged railway strike in 1919, the Ministry of Food asked local Chambers of Commerce to organise the working of motor vehicles primarily for the movement of foodstuffs. The Bolton Chamber set up a committee which met daily

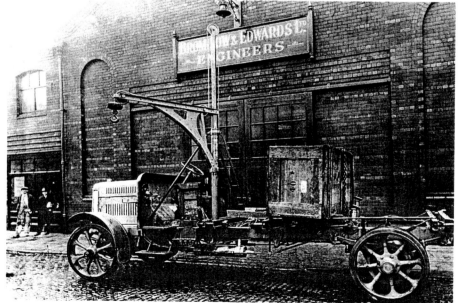

The Anglo-Iranian Oil Company used this solid tyred Leyland for pipe laying. Twin ram tipping gear fittings are at the rear of the packing case and the chassis-mounted crane has a single tipping gear ram for lifting

during the crisis to co-ordinate the movement of goods by road and to ensure a continuing supply of food. After the strike, the advantages of a system of organised road transport were not lost on the Bolton Chamber and they decided to form a Road Transport Clearing House. This was set up in June 1920, following a meeting with Mr Charles Walmsley of the Bolton Transport Agency.

The Bolton Central Transport Agency of Wood Street had begun advertising its services in November 1919. The firm operated as a clearing house for commercial road traffic, finding return loads for vehicles coming into Bolton and acting as a pool for goods to be transported out of the town. Mr Walmsley became the manager of the new clearing house, which was in full operation by September 1920.

In February 1921 there was a meeting with Mr Shaw of the Liverpool Clearing House, who proposed turning the Bolton office into a limited liability company and a subsidiary of the Liverpool operation. The Liverpool clearing house had secured contracts with shipping firms and traffic between the two centres was 'considerably increasing.' The Bolton Chamber of Commerce was initially in favour of the new company, which would have its President on the board, then after further consideration the idea was dropped.

Bolton's transport clearing house became a private concern and the following year was operating from 19 Hotel Street, with Mr Walmsley

An advertisement for the Merrall-Brown cyclecar. The listed distributors could not have made any money, as only 27 were made before the firm closed down in late 1920

the proprietor. The firm advertised efficient and prompt movement of large and small loads, and all goods were insured, whether in transit or in their garage overnight. The customer was charged for only single journeys; the company covered the cost of return trips.

The February 1919 edition of the Light Car and Cyclecar magazine announced 'a newcomer to the motoring world'. The first Merrall-Brown light car, made at Lewis and Bernard Brown's Premier Motor Engineering Co's works on St George's Road, would be ready for the road by the end of the month.

The next edition of the magazine devoted two pages to the car, including photographs and drawings of the 'ingenious' transmission. The engine was an 8hp water-cooled, Y-twin JAP and drive was by chain and sprocket to twin rear wheels set closely together. The body was an attractive two-seater 'with spring cushions' and could be adapted to accommodate a single rear seat in the tail.

Anticipating success for the venture, in August the company advertised for 'high-class tradesmen' such as coach trimmers, fitters, chassis erectors and centre lathe turners... 'Fast and accurate men only need apply.'

In a short article about the car in Autocar magazine for 30th August, the engine was now a two-cylinder, 10hp Precision of 1,096cc with demountable bodies for conversion to passenger carrying if required.

Between April 1919 and November 1920, 120 lorries of various makes in the 1 to 3-ton class were registered. Adding the convertible vehicles in this class brings the total for the period to 151, an indication of the early postwar boom.

A side view of the Merrall-Brown cyclecar. The makers announced proudly that disc wheels were standard and that a spare wheel was included in the equipment

From the details in the registers, it appears that a number of men, probably ex-servicemen, pooled their resources in order to purchase a suitable vehicle. Tom Wilson, Tom Ashton and Tom Walker, trading as Wilson & Co of 29 Empress Street, registered a Lacre convertible lorry BN2884 in January 1919. They must have enjoyed some success, as they registered another new vehicle, a Maudsley convertible BN3815, in March 1920.

In April, William Henry Gregory, Thomas Openshaw, James Hargreaves and James Eastham, trading as GOHE Motors, 241 St Helens Road, registered a Maudsley charabanc BN3830. In May, William Jones, John Holden Ashworth, William Steele, Thomas Sandle and Joseph Sturgess, trading from 48 Fall Birch Road, Horwich, as Horwich Motor Transport, registered an AEC convertible BN4047.

Some firms in the registers are either still in business or survived well into the post 1939-45 period.

Parkside Garage in Peabody Street (Skoda main agents) was established before 1914 and registered a Thornycroft convertible BN2882 in June 1919, followed in July by a Dennis charabanc BN3024, and in March 1920 a Karrier lorry BN3687.

Lee Brothers, old established furniture removers of Darley Street, registered an AEC charabanc BN3019 in July 1919. Fred Snaylam of Ulleswater Street started with a Leyland convertible BN3246 in October 1919, followed by a similar vehicle, BN3942, in April 1920 and another, BN4335, in July 1920.

Arthur Christy of 124 Blackburn Road registered a Leyland convertible BN3737 in March 1920 and grew into one of Bolton's popular coach operators. He had an attractive wooden office and drivers' rest room on Moor Lane bus station, specially designed and built by Roscoe & Sons of Avenue Street.

Hipwood & Grundy was another firm which began in the immediate post 1914-18 War period. Samuel Hipwood and Maurice Grundy of Lord Street, Kearsley, registered an AEC lorry BN3035 in August 1919, followed in January by a Saurer BN3496 (made in Switzerland and imported by Armstrong of Tyneside).

In February 1920 the Central Garage, Victoria Square, was under new management. William Lees of Radcliffe had taken over and it was being equipped with 'a new fleet of char-a-bancs, taxis and touring cars... most up-to-date models in the North of England.'

Prospective day trippers were assured that the charabancs would be for passenger working only, and not used as load carrying vehicles on weekdays. The coachwork, in the 'modern torpedo body design', was by Leyland Motors.

William Lees was originally in Mellor Street, Radcliffe, trading as the Radcliffe Moor Garage. In 1914 he registered a Dennis charabanc BN1731; in 1915 a Belsize

Tillotsons staff outing to Llangollen, assembled on the Town Hall Square. The Bolton Evening News of July 9th 1920 reported that two of the drivers were each fined £5, plus costs, for travelling at 17 and 23mph respectively, when the speed limit was 12mph

convertible lorry BN1954, and in 1916 two Star convertibles, BN2289 and BN2323. Expanding his business in 1919, he added two Leyland convertibles, BN2723 and BN2952, and between April and June 1920 registered a Karrier lorry, BN3881, and two Leyland charabancs, BN4189 and BN4190.

In the field of commercial vehicle sales in 1920, Bromilow & Edwards offered reconstructed Leyland, Karrier, AEC, Thornycroft, Commer, Austin, Fiat and Vulcan lorries with 3-ton and 30cwt capacities. Southerns offered 4-ton Thornycrofts at £1,150, and Walter Bradley, re-entering the trade, had new models of Garner, Lacre, Pagefield, Caledon and Palladium lorries. His address was the Albion Engineering Works, Kingsgate Garage, Central Street.

Stanley Parker announced his entry into the commercial vehicle market in October 1920 as the sole Lancashire and Cheshire distributor for the Whiting lorry in chassis form, ranging from 1 to 2.5 tons and priced at between £450 and £775. Imported from the USA by Whiting (1915) Ltd of London, these could have been the products of seven or eight different makers. Not surprisingly, the firm did not survive into 1921 and, having learned his lesson, Mr Parker kept to the more conventional car and motorcycle makers.

In October 1920 G Graveson & Sons, ironmongers of 141 Market Street, Farnworth, advertised that they were Ford service dealers and could also offer early delivery of Bean cars and Vulcan lorries. The cars came from a Staffordshire firm which did not survive the 1930s crisis in the industry; the lorries may have been the ones built locally by Hick, Hargreaves, a firm better known for the manufacture of steam engines for cotton mills and electricity generating stations.

So what prompted them to venture into the field of petrol engines? The connection may have been motor engineers Walter Bradley and Maurice Edwards, who were both linked with the Vulcan Motor Company of Southport. Vulcan were producing cars and commercials powered mainly by Dorman engines, and perhaps the two engineers decided that a similar engine could be made by a local firm. Just how many Hick, Hargreaves engines were installed in Vulcan vehicles is unknown. There are still some Vulcans in existence, and Bolton awaits news of a locally-produced engine still running in a Vulcan vehicle.

The Bolton School of Motoring at 164 Derby Street was founded about 1918 by Messrs Entwistle & Walker. They began advertising in 1920 and in 1925 were offering a course in

maintenance, troubles and remedies, beginning on 30th September at 7.30pm and continuing 'each Wednesday evening throughout the winter.' It was possible to book for selected items, such as chassis description and petrol engine operation, or for the complete course (£4.4s). The fee for driving tuition, using modern motor cars, was £2.10s and the pupil received 'unlimited instruction until the BSM Certificate granted.'

Government legislation in the post-war period resulted in the formation of the Ministry of Transport in 1919 to replace the Road Transport Board. The Finance Act of 1920 introduced a new system of vehicle taxation: cars up to 5hp would be taxed at £6 per year and for each additional hp there was an extra £1 in tax. The Act confirmed the county and county borough councils as registration authorities and this means of car tax and licensing continued until the Vehicles, Driving and Licensing Act of 1969 transferred the function to the Department of the Environment's central computer system in South Wales.

Once settled down to their peace-time responsibilities, Bolton Corporation decided to spend a bit of ratepayers' money. In February 1920 they agreed to purchase a 30cwt Vulcan tipper for the Gas Department from Bromilow & Edwards. In April it was a motor vehicle for the Electricity Department Fittings Section and also a car for the Supply Department. In June came another Vulcan tipper for the Gas Department, and in July a Lacre motor road sweeper. In October the Watch Committee agreed, subject to a satisfactory medical report by the Fire Brigade surgeon, to appoint James Wilcock as motor engineer for £5 a week. Purchases in 1921 included a steam gulley emptier and a new fire engine, which was displayed on Victoria Square in all its brass finery.

In January 1921 Southerns, seemingly overstocked with motor-cycles, advertised 'shopsoiled' 1920 Levis and Clyno models at less than cost price, 'to make room for 1921

Central Garage, Victoria Square, founded by Thomas Fitton and James Henry Green in 1904, taken over by J B Heaton and T and G Temperley by 1907 and bought by William Lees of Radcliffe in 1920

models.' Another new motor trader, Jim Cottom of 3 Mealhouse Lane, began advertising in January. He dealt in three-wheeled cycle cars, offering 1920 Morgans and two somewhat shortlived mounts, the Bleriot Whippet (made in England between 1920 and 1927) and the Metro-Tyler (made in 1921-23). The following month Albert Horrocks of Horrockses Motor House on Bradshawgate offered Morgan runabouts for £206, finishing his advertisement with an obvious dig at Jim Cottom, 'Real Morgan Specialists.' Mr Cottom seems to have disappeared as quietly as he had arrived in the Bolton motor trade world.

In March 1921 Messrs Aspinall, Simm & Beddows opened their garage in part of the Hulton Coal Depot near Daubhill Station. They claimed to have 17 years' experience in the manufacture and repair of Vulcan cars, which suggests they were former employees of the Vulcan Car Co at Crossens, Southport. John Beddows died in early 1922 when he was electrocuted in the garage pit whilst using a faulty hand lamp connected to the mains. He was only 28 and lived at 326 Halliwell Road.

In June 1921 the Bolton Garage Ltd reported they had moved from 157 Bradshawgate to new and spacious premises in Garside Street. (This later became Hardman & Jacques, then Pilkingtons Garage Ltd, Morris dealers.) The vacated Bradshawgate premises were taken over by Stanley Parker and the site is now occupied by Williams Motor Co, BMW garage and showrooms.

The question of police vehicles occupied quite a bit of Council time during 1921. In February, Bromilow & Edwards were paid £750 for a police car and the Chief Fire Officer submitted plans for a garage for the vehicle. Police motorcycles were discussed in March and in November J V Madgwick was paid £212.8.2d for an AJS model with sidecar. This remained in use until June 1928.

An advertisement for the Church Wharf Garage appeared in

November 1921. The owners, Parker Brothers & Ramsden, said they had twenty years' experience in the trade and 'We served the King well, we can serve you better,' presumably a reference to some form of service during the war. By the 1930s the garage was being run by J T Parker & Sons.

The size and scope of Bromilow & Edwards' business in Bark Street was described in a Bolton Evening News article of November 1921. They had one of the largest motor works 'in the North of England,' with a well-equipped machine shop, spare parts stores, and a 'splendid showroom.' They built, trimmed and painted vehicle bodies and were also haulage and charabanc proprietors. They were the Bolton agents for Vauxhall, Talbot-Darracq and Vulcan, and also dealt in Crossleys, Sentinel steamers, Dodge cars and lorries and cars made by Star of Wolverhampton.

The firm was well established as a maker of hydraulic tipping gears and it did not take long for the twin-ram version to become an important addition to the motor vehicle fleets of road contractors, coal owners and hauliers who specialised in the movement of bulk stone, sand and gravel. The same industries would purchase the next development, the

three-way tipper. This vehicle used the twin-ram assembly to discharge loads to the side or rear with the removal of the appropriate body catches-cum-hinge pins.

There was an unusual addition to Southern Brothers' interests in 1921, when they opened a cinema. The previous year they had purchased an aircraft hangar from a disused airfield in Yorkshire, with the intention of re-erecting it on Higher Bridge Street in Bolton as a garage for their commercial vehicle business. Unfortunately the venture soon failed, leaving the brothers with a large, partly-built structure. A change of plan was needed, so Herbert Southern applied to the Watch Committee for a cinematograph licence. This was granted in May 1921 and the new cinema, the Palladium, opened on Boxing Day 1921 with a showing of a silent melodrama called 'The Old Nest'.

The Southern brothers don't appear to have been involved in the management of the cinema and in 1924 the licence was transferred to a new owner. The former aircraft hangar survived until a few years ago, having been the Wrighton Stadium for all-in wrestling fans and then Skateboard City. When interest in skateboarding waned, the

This model of a Vulcan tipper was displayed by Bromilow and Edwards to attract potential customers

building was demolished and the site is now occupied by Lythgoe Motors Ltd.

In February 1922 Southerns advertised two vehicles which did not have much of a life. The Belsize-Bradshaw two-seater (£275) was fitted with a two-cylinder engine designed by Granville Bradshaw, a somewhat unorthodox engineer, and lasted about three years. The other machine was the French-made De Marcay cyclecar (£175), powered by a 1,000cc Anzani V-twin engine. The makers had been in the aircraft industry and, as this was the era of the spidery and lightweight cycle-cars, they obviously thought they had a winner. The firm did not survive beyond 1922 and how Southerns got involved is something of a mystery.

The popularity of the charabanc for day trips and other excursions led to the formation of the Bolton & District Charabanc Owners Association. In March 1922 the members were:

Abbott & Kershaw, 61 Arkwright Street

H Berry, 143 Sapling Road

W H Bullough & Son, 126 Essingdon Street

Charles T Castle, 291 Radcliffe Road, Darcy Lever

Arthur Christy, 124 Blackburn Road

A Fielding, 456 Blackburn Road

W H Gregory, T Openshaw, J Hargreaves & J Eastham, trading as GOHE Motors, 241a St Helens Road

Holme & Sons, 805 Belmont Road

Holden Brothers, 68 Folds Road

Howarth & Co, 18 Acresfield

W Lees Ltd, Victoria Square & Mellor Street, Radcliffe

F Lomax, 65 Thicketford Road

A & N Lowe, 12 Haigh Street

J Marshall, 66 Noble Street

Parkside Motor Co, Peabody Street

W Pilling, 53 Great Moor Street

T Ramsden & Sons, 87 Ainsworth Lane

F Snaylam, 39 Ulleswater Street

J R Tognarelli, 127 Deansgate

J T Walker & Sons, 252 Deane Church Lane

Walter Wright Motors Ltd, Tonge Bridge

Wilson Motor Haulage, Empress Street

During the summer months the charabancs would line up on the Town Hall Square prior to setting off for various destinations. Following complaints from shopkeepers facing the Town Hall that the vehicles 'formed an unbroken barricade along the front of the shops,' the Watch Committee decided that from June 1922 they should move to the back of the Town Hall, on the north side. At that time, Le Mans Crescent had not been built and Knowsley Street, the Town Hall Square and Newport Street were part of a major tram route through the town, so from a safety point of view it was better to move the charabancs away from where people descended from tramcars.

A traffic census was taken between 8.00am and 8.00pm on 22nd June 1922. The observation points were Manchester Road, Blackburn Road at Astley Bridge, Deane Road, Wigan Road and Chorley New Road. The findings were as follows:

Motorcycles 670. Motor cars 2,715. Motor vans 899. Motor buses and charabancs 87. Motor lorries 3,250. Towed trailers 63. Steam tractors 183. Steam engines 35. Steam trailers 96. Horse vehicles 2,439. Tramcars 2,035. Pedal cycles 2,309. The traffic on Manchester Road was the heaviest, at four vehicles per minute.

In July 1922 a motor car appeared which was destined to become a legend in much the same way as the Ford Model T. This was the Austin Seven, a small, four-seater car with a leatherette hood and a diminutive four-cylinder engine capable of an optimistic 40mph. It was priced at £165 and aimed at the motorcycle fraternity and those who felt that they could just about afford to run a small car for pleasure trips. In December 1922 Southerns advised, 'Don't wait, come and book your order for rotational delivery of an Austin Seven.' In contrast, Gordons advertised the Model T in various forms: vans from £150 to £190, open or closed models from £140 to £160, chassis only £160, truck £185 and farm tractor £225.

At the beginning of 1923 Southerns offered the full range of Austin cars, as well as Buick and Belsize for the average customer, while the more sporting types could go along to the St Georges Road showrooms and admire the new 3-litre Bentley, with its distinctive booming exhaust note from the drainpipe-size exhaust,

A GOHE tour in July 1923: the firm's title came from the initial letters of the proprietors' surnames

and capable of 80mph. For those requiring a more stately means of travel, a Daimler limousine could be supplied, with a 'top hat' body if needed.

At the other end of the scale, Ross Isherwood, licensee of the Prince William Hotel on Bradshawgate and owner of a small garage in Shipgates, could supply a light car called the Stoneleigh, made by Armstrong Siddeley. Costing £185, it was something of a utility vehicle and would seat three plus a small child. Mr Isherwood also advertised, 'All tyre troubles abolished by fitting the everlasting, puncture resisting inner tube.' The make wasn't named, unfortunately.

Walter Bradley opened his new works and showrooms on Deansgate in February 1923. On display were cars from Bean, Fiat, Armstrong-Siddeley, Chevrolet, Oakland, Swift and Bayliss-Thomas (a small two-seater made in Birmingham which faded away before 1930). The firm also dealt in commercial vehicles made by Karrier, Leyland, Lacre and Garner, plus a wide range of electrical appliances.

They would install electric power, heating and lighting in private and commercial premises and the new wireless did not present any difficulty to Walter Bradley's technicians. A large garage was available day and night 'where cars can be left during shopping expeditions, or whilst the owners attend concerts or theatre.' The showroom is now a ladies' dress shop and the garage occupied by other concerns.

Two more garages advertised in the Bolton Evening News: Crawford Motor Bargains of the Haulgh offered second hand cars for sale, and Hulton Motors of Four Lane Ends offered 'Ford Service'. Then in July William Meredith of 'The Garage, Egerton' announced, 'Motorists, when bound for Preston and the North, take the wide, safe and comfortable road through Egerton and fill up at the Golden Pump' - an early example of a roadside filling station.

The 1920s gave birth to component specialists such as Francis & Son, electrical engineers of 231 St Georges Road, who offered a complete accumulator and battery service. Thomas Peake Ltd, 'Radiator Specialist' of Blackbank Street, Astley Bridge, informed the motorist that they were the sole makers of the 'Priceless Patent Silencer' which would give 'More power, less running cost. First and Last Word in Efficiency.' By March 1923 this firm was owned by the silencer patentee, Thomas Price.

The early 1920s was a period of unrest on the railways. Agitation over wage rates was reported in the Bolton Evening News of 31st December 1923 with the announcement, 'Railway Peace in Balance'; union members were awaiting the result of a strike ballot.

The situation prompted Walter Bradley to advise, in January 1924, 'Be Independent of Train Service and Purchase a Car,' and to list his range of vehicles: Fiat, Daimler, Oakland, Bean, etc. Southern Brothers were more direct: 'Railway Strike Latest. Why not be Independent of all Railways, Disputes, etc. Spring is coming and you will probably be thinking of buying a Car then. Why not do it now...'

Bolton Corporation purchased a new 20hp ambulance for £800 in 1924. According to the Bolton Journal of 8th February, it could accommodate two stretchers and four sitting cases, was well sprung and the 'practically noiseless engine ensured a minimum of disturbance of the patients.' It came complete with an illuminated red 'Ambulance' sign. It is more than likely that the vehicle was based on the Austin heavy saloon chassis and supplied by Southerns.

The following month Southerns announced that they were the main distributors for Austin in Bolton, but it did not prevent them from taking up other agencies. In April they advertised the 6-cylinder Essex, a five-seater touring car complete with electric starter, for £350. This was of American origin and marketed as a low-priced saloon.

The 1924 newspapers carried advertisements for cars both popular and obscure. Anyone buying the Navarro 'fast touring car' from Ross Isherwood of Shipgates would have been saddled with an obscure Italian model, but it came from a line of racing cars and no doubt some young Bolton blood would buy it for fast runs over Belmont and on to the coast.

At holiday times, those without a car could embark on a charabanc tour. The Bolton Journal of 16th May 1924 advertised a 700-mile tour of Scotland in seven days for £7.15s, complete with accommodation and 'no extras'. Or 7 days hotel and tours in Ireland could be had for £3.19.6d. Most charabancs were still shod with solid or some form of cushion tyres, but the somewhat bumpy ride was to be expected and generally accepted by those used to the harsh riding of Corporation tramcars.

July 1924 saw the opening salvoes of the battle between Southerns and

Walter Bradley's showroom at the corner of Queen Street and Deansgate in June 1923. He was the local agent for Bean cars, seen far left and next to far right

Parkers over Morris commercial vehicles. Parkers advertised the new Morris 1-ton truck for £225 and they were 'Sole Agents for all Morris products.' In subsequent advertisements, the firm apologised to the Bolton motoring public about delivery of Morris cars; orders were being dealt with in 'strict rotation only'. In early December Southerns announced that they had now been appointed Official Distributors and Main Agent for the district for Morris 1-ton trucks, at £225, £235 and £250.

Southerns had a stand at the 18th Motor Show at Olympia, London, in October 1924. They were advertised as the main Austin distributor for the Bolton district and offered six versions of the 20hp car, from a plain chassis at £395 to the Mayfair Landaulette at £795, and six versions of the Austin 12, from a chassis at £270 to the Berkeley Landaulette at £475. Lower down the scale, the Austin Seven chassis could be had for £120, a saloon for £155, or a 'sports' for £170.

The following month Southerns took on the official agency for Citroen and later in the year became the sole agent for the 'Progress Indicator.' This device acted 'as a rear light and direction indicator automatically,' and at £4.4s supplied and fitted, would be a good Christmas present for the motorist.

In 1924 a very rare car indeed was seen in Bolton. This was the Doble E10 steam car, one of only 45 ever made and at the time the only one in the country. Designed and built by

This photograph of an American Doble steam car E9 in the Ford Company's Museum in the USA is almost identical with Mr Bentley's E10, last seen in 1935 in London. The E10's subsequent fate is uncertain

Abner Doble, a Californian engineer, the car was fuelled by paraffin and had a 17-gallon water tank, which was sufficient for 'over a hundred miles,' depending on how it was driven. It was started with an ignition key and took between a minute and a minute-and-a-half to reach working pressure in the boiler. A maximum speed of between 90 and 100mph was claimed.

Bolton's owner of the Doble was Mr Bentley, a manager at John Musgrave & Son, steam engineers. When this firm collapsed in 1926 he moved to the York area, taking the car with him. A few years later Abner Doble was in England, acting

as consultant to the Sentinel Steam Wagon Co, and he saw Mr Bentley's car again in York in 1933. The last registration had expired in December 1928 and there were 12,914 miles on the clock.

During 1924, 2,088 licences for private cars had been taken out in Bolton, 393 more than 1923. The figure for motorcycles was 2,133 (up by 229) and for commercials 1,532 (up by 144). This steady increase was reflected in the wide range of newspaper advertisements in 1925.

Southerns were quick off the mark, reminding the public they were the Morris 1-ton truck distributors and also agents for the Thornycroft 30cwt 'Subsidy Type' chassis at £360. Competitors in this respect were Messrs Hardman & Jacques of Garside Street, who were sole district agents for 30cwt to 3-ton Guy truck chassis. They also offered a French car, the Mathis 9hp four-seater, in competition with Southerns' Citroen. The Mathis started as a German car made in Strasbourg, Alsace, which became part of France after the 1914-18 war.

The same firm were agents for one of Scotland's cars, the Galloway, built by Arroll-Johnson at their factory in Dumfries. In 1916 the firm

Bolton blind persons' picnic in 1924. Note the 'cushion' type of solid tyres on the front wheels; these made travel over setts a bit more comfortable

built a new works, the Galloway Engineering Co, at Tongland, Kirkcudbright, which was staffed mainly by women. The employment of women on munitions and in engineering during the war was widespread, but the manager, Mr T C Pullinger, took it a step further when he envisaged a fully trained engineering staff of women drawn from the upper echelons of society. In November 1917 he took an advertisement in The Lady magazine, offering apprenticeships at Tongland for 'educated and refined women who have a taste for mathematics and mechanics.' The works amenities included a rooftop tennis court, a rest room with piano and a swimming pool. The kitchen 'would rejoice the heart of the most fastidious housewife.'

When the war ended, Arroll-Johnson decided to produce a small car at Tongland based on the Fiat 501. Mr Pullinger's daughter, Dorothea, who had been in charge of women workers at Vickers, Barrow-in-Furness, during the war, became the manager. The Galloway car was produced at Tongland between 1919 and 1921, when production was transferred to Dumfries and the unique workforce was disbanded.

In early 1925 a Mr Hennessy of 1 Castle Street offered his bodywork services to Bolton motorists. Hoods could be re-covered, side curtains provided and leather hoods were a speciality. By March 1925 Hennessy's garage was at 137 High Street, Daubhill, where they would attend to hoods, side curtains and upholstery. They could also supply Auster rear windscreens, fitted behind the front seats to give some protection to the passengers.

Garages advertising for what seems to have been the first time included Hodges & Knowles, based in part of the Kings Hall Buildings at the corner of Breightmet Street and Bradshawgate, and the Kershaw Motor Co of Moss Bank Way, Smithills, who announced they were sole agents in Bolton for Chevrolet cars. Walter Pilling, formerly a cycle maker at Eagley, was 'the local Riley agent' at Kapstan House, Great

Moor Street. Arnold Kay of 143-145 Bradshawgate advertised the Buick, an American car from an 'entirely British part of GMC.'

The International Motor Co of St Georges Road offered two models of Trojan, a tourer on pneumatic tyres at £130 and a 7cwt van on solids at £125. This rather unusual, simple and robust vehicle had its engine horizontally under the driver's seat, chain drive to one rear wheel and braking on the other wheel.

In May, Hardman & Jacques took on the Jowett agency, offering a 2-seater for £152. This car, made at Idle, near Bradford, was a good little vehicle for its day, and considered a bit more upmarket than the Trojan. Also in May, the Auto & Engineering Co of Newport Street announced they were Salmson distributors. This open two-seater was French-built, in rakish style, and would cost the sporting motorist £158.

After the 1914-18 war Bolton Corporation embarked on a major road building project to create a ring road round part of the town, starting at Wigan Road and ending at Bury Road. The first section to be completed was Beaumont Road, between Wigan and Chorley New Roads, and it was opened by the Minister of Transport on 18th June 1925. A few days earlier the Bolton Motor Cycle Club organised a programme of events for

motorcycles and cars. It was well advertised, and an estimated crowd of 15,000 spectators lined both sides of the road. Unfortunately, in the opening event a motorcycle rider lost control of his machine at 70mph, ran into the gutter and killed 15-year-old Thomas Mulrooney of Westhoughton. The Club President, Councillor Walter Bradley, immediately cancelled the event.

In July 1925 Horrockses Motor House, Bradshawgate, agents for Singer cars, waxed lyrical: 'Thousands of Throats Chorus the Singer Song.' This make of car dated from 1905 until 1956, when it became part of the Rootes Group, and finally disappeared in the early 1970s. A few doors down Bradshawgate, Arnold Kay advertised the Bentley 3-litre in chassis form at £925. If something grander was required, the 6-litre chassis was £1,450. For the complete car, the prices would be doubled.

The war of words over Morris commercial vehicles began to warm up in September 1925. Southerns announced that from 14th September every 1 ton and 12cwt Morris commercial sold 'Will have a maintenance allowance providing free repairs, upkeep and adjustments.' All models would be fitted with an engine-driven tyre pump and a 'Thermit Heat Controlling Device' (probably some form of thermostat in the engine cooling system).

Before its official opening as part of the new Ring Road, Beaumont Road was used for motor-cycle races, organised by Councillor Walter Bradley, a leading motor trader; he is the one in bowler hat and wing collar standing between the two cyclists at the front

In October, concerned about 'certain misleading advertisements,' Morris Commercial Cars Ltd itself was moved to place a notice in the papers, confirming Southerns as their only sales and service agent in Bolton. Morris Commercial was a separate part of the Morris organisation, but this was never made clear in the various advertisements; a few days later an announcement from Pilkingtons of Turk Street contained the words, 'The Original Morris Agents.' Parkers weighed in with, 'Why not place your order direct with the Largest District Suppliers and secure all the advantages of a transaction with the most complete Morris Organisation in this part of the country?' Pilkingtons hit back with a list of reasons why anyone wanting a Morris car should come to them. They were the sales and service agents, they always had a representative stock of current models and the best stock of Morris parts for miles around, and they had a reputation for satisfaction. Eventually the matter settled down, with Southerns concentrating on Austin vehicles and Parkers with a variety of passenger cars, leaving Pilkingtons a clear field with Morris.

A December 1925 advertisement gives some idea of Parkers' range of cars. In a list of 34 'shop soiled and second-hand' models, as well as the mundane Austin, Ford and Morris, there were Hispano-Suiza, Crossley, Sunbeam, Talbot-Darracq, Humber, Standard, Bean, Calthorpe, Singer, Overland, Wolseley, Swift and Essex, plus a locally-made Merrall-Brown, 2-seater 1921 model, for £50.

Towards the end of the year Kershaws of Moss Bank Way began to advertise Chevrolet commercials: Milk Van £149, Carrier's Lorry £203 and Delivery Van £208. Two days later they announced that a Bolton Chevrolet carrying over one ton daily had covered 1,200 miles in one month, at a cost of 1.09d per mile for oil and petrol. No other costs were incurred. The next advertisement included the verse:

'There's a Chev for every purpose,
A few drops will run a mile,
Those left behind may curse us,
But we go on - and smile.'

Gordons - the Formative Years to 1927

This thriving motor trader is the oldest in Bolton still governed by members of the founder's family. The origins can be traced back as far as 1820, when John Croall began a coachmaking business in Edinburgh; one of his employees was Samuel Gordon (I). According to an interview made for 'The Garage and Motor Trader' in December 1943 with Samuel Gordon (III), Samuel Gordon (I) left Edinburgh in 1823 and set off for Bolton as a young journeyman coach-builder. The article stated that he lived to be over 90 and saw his son, Samuel (II), found his own business in Bolton in 1863. Samuel Gordon (II) died in January 1935.

In 1823 Bolton was expanding in engineering, textiles and coal, and Samuel Gordon (I) could have found employment with one of two coach-builders: Joseph Cooper of Bradshawgate or T C Wordell of nearby Blackburn Street.

A year later, a local directory only listed Joseph Cooper and two coach proprietors advertising their services: coaches left three public houses in the town for Edinburgh via Preston, Kendal and Glasgow,

and other coaches went to London, Manchester and the Midlands.

In 1831 a railway line was in operation between Bolton and Liverpool via the Bolton-Leigh-Kenyon Junction and linked with the Liverpool-Manchester Railway. The coaches for the Bolton Railway had been made by Joseph Cooper, so it is quite possible that the young journeyman Samuel Gordon (I) played a part in their construction and painting. A report on this railway in 1838 states that there were six 24-seater first class coaches with the insides fitted with blue cloth and painted green with the arms of the company emblazoned on the panels; each cost £400. There were also eight second class coaches of a more utilitarian interior.

Samuel Gordon (II) (1846-1935) clearly left Bolton at some point to further his experience and craftsmanship, for after his return, an advertisement in the 1881 Bolton Directory stated that he had had considerable experience in the leading firms in England, giving him 'a thorough knowledge of the Trade.'

Gordon's works, photographed about 1904, with a cab in the side street seemingly waiting for its horse and a motor car (make unknown) in front

The 1943 interview stated that Samuel (I) helped Samuel (II) to found his Bolton coachworks, but did not say exactly where, so it is difficult to determine, as there are no references in any of the early street directories. The Poor and District Ratebooks in Bolton Archives do have an entry 'Workshop Saml. Gordon Payment £1.14.0' in Falcon Street in February 1879, but the 1874-78 volumes showing Falcon Street occupants do not list him.

His obituary in the Bolton Evening News of 28th January 1935 states that he was in his 89th year, had come from Birmingham as a young journeyman carriage builder and had founded his business '60 years previous'. This would give a foundation date within four years of the first reference in 1879 to Falcon Street. The 1863 date given in the 1943 interview seems slightly suspicious, as this was the period of the American Civil War, from which the textile trade suffered badly, so there was extensive distress in the manufacturing districts. Perhaps not a good time for starting a new carriage-making business? We may never know where the business was

started, but so far, Falcon Street seems the most likely candidate.

The 1881 directory does list Samuel Gordon (II) with other coach-builders: Fred Welman & Co, Manor Street, Henry Julian, Bow Street and Roberts Brothers of Nelson Square; the last firm also had premises in Haworth Street, but five minutes' walk from Samuel Gordon's works. The 1882 5ft:1 mile Survey shows Roberts' coachworks and an outline of Samuel Gordon's in Falcon Street; the 1908 25inch:1 mile Survey shows only the latter. The Roberts Brothers do not seem to have been involved with the motor vehicle and closed down in the early 1900s; the place was used by other industries until after World War Two, when it disappeared during extensive reconstruction of the area.

An early photograph of Samuel Gordon's new premises, with an impressive frontage on to Higher Bridge Street, bears the title 'Coachworks' in prominent letters over the upper floor; a later one (still pre-1914) shows this now to be 'Motor Car Works'. Whilst details of early vehicles constructed by Samuel Gordon (II) have yet to be

discovered, in November 1905 he tendered for a horse-drawn ambulance for Bolton Corporation. This was accepted and completed in April 1906, the Watch Committee paying £89.5.0d and a further £12.7.0d for a set of harness.

In August 1907 the Royal Lancashire Show was held on land in Green Lane, Great Lever. Amongst the exhibitors was, according to the Bolton newspapers, 'Mr. Samuel Gordon, coachbuilder and Motor-Car Works, a double seated Brougham, luxuriously trimmed in black satin and gold lace, and fitted with electric lights, also a double landaulet motor body with the latest pattern S.C.A.T. Italian chassis for Mr.H.L.Rushton of Dobson and Barlows. There is also a Dupont Victoria besides a number of Ralli cars and Liverpool Gigs and Governess cars' - quite an impressive display for the firm.

At the Manchester Show in February 1911 he exhibited a 22hp Daimler for a 'Local Gentleman'; the Bolton papers did not expand on this item. Altogether these shows indicate a successful transition towards the motor car whilst still

Inside Gordon's garage before 1914; possibly a Daimler or Panhard limousine under repair. Note that the car is held up by a chain block and resting on the pit boards. A large gearbox is also being repaired

catering for established clientele in the horse world.

The Bolton Motor Vehicle Registers in Bolton Archives show that Samuel Gordon had registered a new 2.5hp Vulcan car, BN153, on 28th October 1904, when he was living at 7 Hilden Street - at that time the preferred local area for many up-and-coming successful businessmen. On 16th February 1911 Samuel's wife, Sarah, became the owner of a 12hp White steam-car, BN325; this was originally registered new to Thomas Jackson of Heaton on November 11th 1906. On 15th April 1911 Samuel Gordon moved to a higher class of car when he registered, new, a 30/34hp Daimler landaulette, BN643.

By this time a separate garage had been added in nearby Edmund Street and from the middle of 1909 he advertised in the nationwide magazine 'The Autocar': 'Gordon's, Bridge Street Automobile Engineers and Garage, Telephone 798, All Repairs. I P (Inside Parking), Charging (Batteries), Vulcanising (Tyre Repairs), Michelin and Goodrich Tyres, Bolton, Lancs.'

An advertisement in the Bolton Evening News of 15th March 1996 suggests that Gordons were Ford agents as early as 1912. In June 1903 Henry Ford had founded the Ford Motor Company to produce the Model A with its flat-twin 8hp engine, two of which were imported into Great Britain in 1904. It is understood that one Percival Perry

was involved in this matter. About that time the Central Motor Car Company was founded in London with a licence to sell Ford cars for a period of five years, but this arrangement ended in 1910 when Ford Motor Company (England) was formed, with Percival Perry as its head.

By this time Ford had produced B, C, F, K, P and S, all leading to the famous Model T with its two-pedal and hand brake lever control of forward gears, a separate pedal for reverse and a hand throttle to control speed, the mechanism based on epicyclic gears requiring no actual gear movement by the driver. First produced in 1908, this was later imported into Great Britain and its success led the Ford Motor Company to open a works at Trafford Park, Manchester, with Percival Perry as manager, in 1911.

The first Model T Ford registered in Bolton was BN556, classed as a 20/24hp model, on 9th April 1910 to local motor trader Isaiah Dootson of Bridgeman Street. A second, BN592 on 13th July 1910, was for G Holden of Fishergate, Preston. As the Trafford Park Works did not produce any cars until 1911, these two must have come to Bolton during the formative years of the Works. Whether Samuel Gordon was involved in buying them is not known, but once production began, more Model T vehicles began to arrive and between 1st August 1911 and 1st May 1912 eleven had appeared, plus a chocolate-coloured van, registered BN858 on 13th March 1912 to a Thomas Browne of 'Mondsfield', Bromley Cross; this was the first commercial-bodied Model T in Bolton.

It was the practice then for garages to hold agencies for a variety of

A motor engineer working on an early screw-cutting lathe in Gordon's garage. Note the electrical switchgear and lights on the wall

vehicles. In November 1915 Southern Brothers (Austin dealers) were official agents for Ford and Dodge vehicles, and in January 1918 Gordons were offering 'Austin Cars - Early Delivery'. In November 1919 Gordons were paid £585 for 'Motor-Lorries' by Bolton Corporation, who also resolved to purchase a Ford motor-car for 'Committee Use'. This did not stop Gordons accepting the sole agency for the Scottish made Beardmore cars, but this seems to have been short-lived, and Gordons began to concentrate on Fords, private and commercial.

A further step forward came on 19th December 1923, when the Watch Committee allowed Gordons to store 500 gallons of petrol in an underground tank near the Falcon Street works. This would have been a 'package deal' of the system patented by Silvanus Freelove Bowser of Fort Wayne, Indiana. It included a hand cranked pump dispenser which filtered the petrol as it was being delivered, and a pointer on a circular scale displayed the amount; this could be zeroed when delivery ended and a cumulative counter was included for the garage accounts.

By the middle of 1926 the Ford Model T commercial vehicle was becoming a bit dated and had a serious rival in the Morris 1 tonner, so Gordons set about extolling the virtues of the Model T. An advertisement in July stated, 'On account of the excessive weight and consequent damage to roads, all Ton lorries other than Fords will be taxed at £26 from January 1923 - Fords £16.' (The difference in rate is because the tax system at the time was based on horsepower.) In September, they announced, '1 ton Ford truck, £112 and tax £16, Insurance £8', and in November, 'Estimate for a Model T running costs:- Complete 1 ton truck 18cwt 2quarters. "Others"... 22cwt. Estimate... 8.5cwt load @6d a mile. On 500 mile average per annum £125. Extra for licence £10. Insurance £7.' The reduced licence and insurance costs were possibly a sales discount.

In August 1927 production of the Ford Model T in cars and commercial forms ceased, having reached 15,000,000 world wide. It was replaced later that year with the Model A in both car and van forms, plus a chassis only for individual

bodyworks; there was also a slightly larger truck chassis, Model AA. Thus ended the first phase of Ford association with Samuel Gordon, but many years with subsequent products were to come.

Among these was the Fordson farm tractor. About 1920 the Bolton papers advertised for customers for the new Model F form, priced at £225; this also created a new department of Gordons.

This model was the result of Ford's experiments begun in 1906/7, with an emphasis on low cost and high volume production. The original engine and transmission were based on the Ford Model B and had been designed by a Hungarian-born engineer, Joseph Galamb. Further experiments resulted in another Hungarian-born engineer, Eugene Farkas, designing a variation which impressed Henry Ford so much that he authorised a batch of 50 to be produced for field trials. This became the basis for the Model F. It had a 20hp petrol/paraffin engine with four cylinders, giving, at 1,000rpm of the engine, 1.5mph in first gear, 2.75mph in second and 6.75 in direct top. It had iron wheels with strakes on the larger rears, and also it did not have any brakes!

The Society of Motor Manufacturers and Traders and the Royal Agricultural Society of Great Britain held a farm tractor trial near Lincoln between 28th September and 7th October 1920. Of 46 entrants in 7 classes, 38 completed the trial, including the Ford Model F. It completely satisfied the judges as to its ploughing, but did not qualify for an award as it did not comply with the rules regarding brakes - all other entrants had some form of built-in brake system. Nevertheless, 500,000 Model Fs had been produced by 1925 in the USA and Cork, Ireland.

In 1927 a road-going model was produced at the Ford Trafford Park Works, which did have a transmission brake in the drive line and solid rubber tyres.

Gordon's were still involved in this aspect of the business until at least the mid-1960s, when the writer contacted them for information about Fordson tractors.

The Fordson farm tractor modified for road use, with solid rubber tyres on all wheels and the transmission altered to include a brake. The driver is believed to be a youthful Dick Rigby, one of Gordon's mechanics and later foreman and service manager

The Bolton Motoring Scene 1926-1930

Kershaws of Moss Bank Way must have made a New Year's resolution to embark upon a serious attack on the light lorry market. On January 4th they announced that a Chevrolet truck could take a load to Blackburn, Oldham or Preston 'in top gear at 20mph, engine rpm 1,000, oil consumption 3,000mpg.' Two days later they stated that a Bolton Chevrolet lorry had run for two years without any repairs and had not even had a spark plug removed. Running costs worked out at '15 miles for 1/-.' The following day they stated that one of their lorries would travel 'up Thicketford Road in Top Gear.' Crompton Way had not been completed at that time and the hill was a local test of ability.

In February Kershaws were advertising Chevrolet cars. Regarding the five-seater saloon at £199, they stated, 'Regret no ashtray, but suggest if you smoke a good brand you would be at your destination before you needed one.'

The other main agents continued to advertise their wares. As well as 'All Bentley models from £999 to £2,500,' Arnold Kay offered six-cylinder Oldsmobiles between £279 and £335, and Lea-Francis sports cars between £260 and £370. On display in Walter Bradley's Deansgate showroom was a 14hp Bean car which had travelled across Australia twice and then won a silver medal in the Lands End to John o'Groats rally.

In 1926 Southerns introduced a cartoon character to their advertisements. 'Appy Andy' was of a sporting disposition and dressed accordingly, in check cap, matching plus-fours and a plaid sports jacket. He was depicted giving the thumbs-up sign with a cheerful smile. In July, after the Bolton Holidays, he took a dig at hikers who made for the open countryside: 'Don't gasp and perspire up hills on Shanks' Pony. It's healthier and far more comfortable in a Clyno, 45mpg, for £162.10s.'

In April 1926 the Bolton Evening News carried a report entitled 'Road Monsters on Trial,' concerning the inspection of 41 charabancs licensed to operate in Bolton. At that time, motor coaches and charabancs were classed as Hackney carriages under the 1904 Act, so annual examination and issue of the appropriate licences were the responsibility of the local authority.

The Hackney Carriage Inspector 'gave a good character to each of the charas,' the Chief Constable examined the door fastenings and the 'grand jury' of 23 men checked the condition and mechanical fitness of the machines, which were then free to 'embark as soon as they wished on the work of carrying Bolton into the fresh air.'

One of the vehicles was new and had to be subjected to a fully laden road test by a 'common jury', which involved filling every seat with a passenger. It soon became known among the spectators on Moor Lane that a free ride was available and about twelve climbed aboard. The charabanc set off under the charge of the Inspector, halting at the corner of Deansgate and Bradshawgate, where 'a shoal of volunteers' filled the vacant seats.

On a fairly level stretch of Bury Road between Churchgate and Tonge Bridge the Inspector ordered what was apparently an emergency stop. The vehicle 'stood in its tracks,' and it must have been quite a noisy and rough affair, with solid tyres on cast steel wheels rattling on the standard granite setts. They then headed for Thicketford Road, with its 1 in 6 gradient and short section of 1 in 5. The driver had to pull up quickly, using hand and foot brakes together and then each brake singly, both going up and coming down the hill. Next they headed for Ainsworth, where the 'narrow and rutted lane of Cockey Moor' was a test of steering and suspension. The vehicle survived and the driver thankfully headed back to Moor Lane.

In April 1926 Bromilow & Edwards announced a special demonstration week of Vulcan cars and commercial vehicles. By then the firm's standard and three-way tipper designs were well established and after some experiments, Maurice Edwards produced the first high-lift tipper. This vehicle could be used as a normal, rear hinged tipper or the whole tipper body could be raised vertically and the load tipped from a greater height. This was especially useful in the coal yards of mills and works, where coal could be stacked to a greater height without the use of conveyors.

A three-way tipper outside the Thynne Street works of Bromilow & Edwards

In the summer of 1926 Messrs Reilly & Brookes of Daubhill opened a store at 11 Great Moor Street for the distribution of Bosch & Mea magnetos, Exide starting and lighting batteries, and other automotive electrical accessories. The Priceless Patent Silencer Works in Blake Street advised the commercial vehicle world that War Department and Admiralty vehicles were fitted with their products, which were also 'standard equipment of most vehicle manufacturers.' The Verts Indicator Co of Clifton Street, off the bottom of Vernon Street, was marketing an indicator device. This comprised an illuminated arm fixed to the top of the dashboard, which the driver moved to show the person in front which way he intended to turn. There was an electrical connection between the arm and a box at the rear of the car, with illuminated arrows to indicate a left or right turn to the vehicle behind.

In September Booths Motors of Philip Street recommended that 'Clerks and Assistants' contact them regarding a special offer, in the form of winter season classes in bus driving. There were 'special terms for ladies' and it would be interesting to know whether any ladies took the course and became bus drivers before the 1939-45 war.

Other advertisers included Hodges & Knowles of Breightmet Street (Kings Hall Buildings), who said they could make bumpers for any car; £4 for a front and rear set. In early November Pilkingtons announced that they now had a showroom at the corner of St Edmund Street and Deansgate. They continued to advertise their Turk Street works offering Ford parts for sale, aluminium radiators for £3, rear axle assemblies £3 and Ford engine overhauls for £8.

In December 1926 'Yankee Jack Bennion, the World's Master Welder' advertised his arrival in Bolton. His address was 37a Blackburn Road and his expertise covered 'Cylinders, crankcases, gearboxes, chassis, etc, scientifically welded. Every job guaranteed and finished equal to new.' In his last advertisement of the year he gave himself the title, 'The Wizard of the Torch.'

The year 1927 opened with Southern Brothers offering a free ride in a Clyno during 'Clyno Invitation Week.' The response seems to have been minimal, as they announced a few days later, 'So far fewer than 50 people have taken advantage - don't be bashful - there's no obligation.' The Clyno company made a small car in

competition with Morris and at one time it was the third largest car maker in the country. It failed in 1929 after a cost-cutting war between the two makers.

Among the new ventures advertised in the early part of 1927 were Reilly & Brookes, now offering services for dynamos and magnetos at 11 Great Moor Street, and S H Motors, auto engineers of Station Garage, Moses Gate. Messrs Gray & Sons of the Bolton Trailer Works, Scholey Street, Manchester Road, advertised 'All Steel Trailers, four wheeled, drawbar, weight 22cwt and guaranteed to carry 4 tons.' In February, 'Yankee Jack' continued his self-aggrandising announcements: 'Bolton born and trained, but with 15 years experience on 3 Continents, recognised as the World's Master Welder.' Later in the month Samuel Haslam, wheelwright and smith of Eldon Street, Tonge Moor, offered to build 'Commercial Motor Bodies of Every Description.'

In March and April the local dealers advertised various cars for sale in the spring. Arnold Kay had Buicks from £398 to £725 and Parkers had the new 6-cylinder Chrysler, with 'hydraulic brakes on all wheels' and a 'vibrationless engine.' H Whitehead & Co at the Bolton Road Garage, Edgworth, were agents for two and four-seater Cluley saloons. Buyers of these would not have been too pleased when the firm closed down the following year. Hardman & Jacques of Garside Street offered the Jowett for between £139 and £185, and Bromilow & Edwards, competing with Parkers and Arnold Kay in the American car market, advertised the Erskine Studebaker for £295, 'spare tyre and bumpers £12.10s extra.'

Auto & Engineering of Newport Street still catered for sporting types with the Salmson Sports Special at £165. Or for £275 there was the Weyman saloon, which had a wooden frame and leatherette covered body. All the wooden joints were separated by shaped metal plates to cut down the body creaks and give some degree of flexibility over the rough roads of the time.

A double, high-lift tipper belonging to Bradford Colliery Company seen in action

Car repairers advertising in April included the Endon Street Garage, Chorley Old Road, 'Star Auto Engineers and Essex Specialists,' William Meredith of Blackburn Road, Egerton, and Wrights Arms Garage, Belmont, which was an RAC approved agent: 'If in trouble, send for the RAC relief car.' H A Peat of the Cricket Ground Garage, Green Lane, undertook repairs and had a car for hire for weddings and other functions.

The exploits of young motorcyclists sometimes resulted in an appearance in the local Magistrates' Court. In May 1927 William Connor of Moorland Grove was stopped by the police as he was going up Markland Hill Lane. He was sitting on the tank and had two girl passengers, one on the saddle and the other on the rear mudguard. He was also accused of not having his front acetylene lamp lit. In his defence, he said he was 'making for the nearest gas lamp to light it.' He was fined £2.5s.

Advertising the Austin range about this time, Southern Brothers stated, 'Austin cars can embody everything that is reliable. Full of power, liveliness and comfort. Remarkably smooth in action and noted for their amazing long lives. From the efficient little Seven to the Majestic Twenty, Austin cars command respect throughout the Motoring World.' On 5th July they proudly announced that an Austin Seven had travelled from Lands End to Bolton in 12 hours 10 minutes at 50mpg. Considering the state of the roads at the time, it was quite an achievement.

One wonders whether the driver took advantage of Preston's (the Deansgate jewellers) 'Prestolee Trunk'. This could be made to fit any body contour and matched to the colour of the car. It would go in the boot or on the drop-down rear luggage grid, a standard fitting on most cars of the day.

At the end of July the Royal Lancashire Agricultural Society held its annual show in a field adjacent to Beaumont Road, giving local motor traders the opportunity to display

their commercial models. Bromilow & Edwards had their tippers, and Gordons had Model T Ford light vans and trucks. Walter Bradley had Bean and Overland, an American vehicle produced at Crossleys of Gorton, and Kershaws Motors displayed a range of Chevrolet trucks. Auto & Engineering presented the Laffley as a chassis at £495, for both passenger and commercial body fitting. This was of French origin and survived until 1953.

The roadside garage-cum-filling station had become an established feature of main roads by the mid-1920s and they ranged from the ornate to simple brick or timber outhouses attached to the owner's residence. The situation prompted the Minister of Transport to sponsor a competition announced in the Bolton Evening News in September 1927. There were prizes for winning designs of the 'ideal country garage,' part of a scheme to 'prevent disfigurement of the countryside by ugly wayside garages.'

Also in September, the annual report of the Inspection of Buses and Taxis stated that there were only seven horse-drawn cabs left in Bolton. Only one of these regularly plied for hire; the others were licensed by a firm of coach proprietors 'for rush hour work as required.' The firm could well have been Messrs Holdens.

The introduction of some form of driving test was discussed at the annual banquet of the Motor Agents' Association in London and duly reported in the Bolton Evening News in October.

According to the principal speaker, Viscount Curzon, about 4,000 people were killed in motor accidents each year in this country and a voluntary driving test leading to a Government certificate would help to reduce this number. The AA did not agree and proposed that drivers, when obtaining licences, 'should be put on their honour to observe the rules of the road, and also to declare that they are physically fit to drive a car.'

Among the traders advertising in the local press at this time were Walker's Union Plating Works, located 'behind Smith's Piano Shop' on Bradshawgate. They offered a cure-all additive called Zoll-Peer which 'saves 35% in cost of petrol' and 'increases mileages by 50%.' The Bolton motorist was advised to 'Investigate this. It's true, not a dud, but an engineer's discovery.'

'Yankee Jack' was still promoting himself in November: 'Sheffield metallurgical experts say he is the leading authority on Autogenous Welding.' (A method of sheet metal welding with the minimum amount of welding rod usage.)

A six-wheeled conversion flat-bed truck operated by Barlow Brothers, Worsley Road, Farnworth, carrying a good load of freshly made wooden packing cases

One of the latest trends in commercial vehicle design was discussed in the Bolton Evening News in mid-November. This was the three-axle, six-wheel layout, which gave an increased carrying capacity for goods or passengers. A German firm, Bussing, had produced a three-axle chassis in 1923 and by 1927 so had Karrier, Caledon, Thornycroft, Leyland and Sentinel (a steamer). A Chevrolet six-wheeler was advertised by Kershaws of Moss Bank Way for £286.

In 1926 or 1927 Maurice Edwards and Albert Horrocks, a co-director of Bromilow & Edwards, purchased the Royal Ruby Works in Altrincham and set about designing a cheap-to-run cyclecar. Under the title 'A New Three-Wheeler', the Motor Cycle magazine for 27th October 1927 described 'Three Interesting Royal Ruby Models.' One had a 343cc Villiers two-stroke engine and transmission via chains and a 3-speed Sturmey-Archer gearbox to a single rear wheel. The second had a single-cylinder 596cc JAP engine and the third a twin Blackburne engine. A reporter for the Light Car and Cyclecar

William Brimelow's mid-1920s advert relating to tyres and services at his Manchester Road depot, opposite Orlando Bridge. Note the smartly dressed salesman with his tie and wing collar

magazine saw a prototype with the Blackburne engine at a motorcycle show at Olympia. The general layout was 'practical and workmanlike,' but he had reservations about the chain transmission.

The Royal Ruby cyclecar did not go into production and in 1928, after being redesigned by Maurice Edwards, it emerged as the MEB (Maurice Edwards Bolton). This was based on the Blackburne engine model and 'a car-type gearbox,' so perhaps Maurice took notice of the reporter's comments on chain transmission.

In 1927, within an area bounded by St Georges Road, Moor Lane, Burnden, Tonge Fold and Churchbank, there were 21 garages offering their services to Bolton motorists, plus two fairly large tyre concerns, Thistlethwaites of Burns Street and William Brimelow of Manchester Road. Outside these boundaries, another 45 medium and one-man concerns were spread across the borough, some of them running taxi-cabs. Thomas Relph of Blackbank Street advertised 'smart taxis, weddings a speciality.' Ross Isherwood had 'Superior private motors for hire' at the Prince William Hotel, Bradshawgate, and Hodkinson & Bleakley of 144 Tonge Moor Road were 'cycle repairers and taxi-cab owners.' Horwich had five garages and one, John Slack of 345 Chorley New Road, was well up to date, being a 'motor engineer and wireless engineer.'

A garage opened at the junction of the recently completed Beaumont Road and Wigan Road in January 1928. Proprietor John T Greenall informed all that he was agent for Bayliss-Thomas light cars and Calthorpe, Dunelt and Excelsior motorcycles. He also said he had garage facilities for 50 cars and the reason for this is not clear. The garage was on the edge of the countryside next to Deane Colliery (now Barton Grange Garden Centre) and the miners of the day did not run cars.

Also in January, the firm of Oscar T Baker, electric motor rewinder, became Baker Brothers and motor

vehicle electrics was added to their range of services at 23 Hanover Street. In poetic vein, they advised, 'If your motors play you tricks, And you find you are in a fix, Ring up Bolton Four Four Six.'

At the end of January the Chief Constable, Mr Mullineux, expressed his concern about motorists 'gutter crawling' and 'enticing young girls into cars and then off to Doffcocker, Smithills Dean and Walker Fold Road.' He was determined to stamp it out and was considering introducing motor patrols.

Advertisers in the early part of 1928 included a new firm, Parkinson & Wilson of 57 Partridge Street, Moor Lane. They offered 'mudguards in silver steel from £3 per set, enamelling or coach painting extra.' Pillings of Great Moor Street had the new Citroen 12/24hp, 'fitted with every conceivable accessory.' Walter Pilling, a former cycle maker, had joined the rapidly expanding band of road transport operators just after the 1914-18 war, when he purchased five Maudsley charabancs.

With a view to competing with the Bolton Motor Co and Pilkingtons, Gordons, Ford main dealer, opened a showroom in part of the Fire Station buildings at the corner of Deansgate and St Edmund Street.

In April 1928 Reilly & Brookes were urging motorists to purchase a 'North East Horn and be on the safe side.' This seems to have been a near relation to the foghorn, as it was described as having a clear and commanding tone, and it cost £1.7.6d. An advertisement for Southerns at this time appealed to the patriotic: 'Austin Cars - as Reliable as the Union Jack - and British.'

Stanley Parker announced in July 1928 that he was the sole agent for Austin and Morris cars fitted with Swallow coachwork, a move which eventually led to Parkers becoming main agents for SS and Jaguar cars.

The Swallow company was formed in Blackpool in 1922 as the Swallow Sidecar Co. It was owned by William Walmsley and William

Lyons and their sidecars, reminiscent of a Zeppelin in shape, became very popular in the 1920s-30s. According to an account of the early days of Jaguar cars written by Andrew White in 1980, William Lyons obtained an Austin Seven chassis from Stanley Parker in 1927 and on this Lyons built a saloon body of his own design. In 1929 an Austin-Swallow two-seater was a class winner of the Southport Concours d'Elegance and a photograph in the Jaguar book shows Stanley Parker holding the trophy.

In the mid-1920s the Bolton motorcyclist could go along to Charlie Robinson in Higher Bridge Street or Syl Anderton in Bridgeman Place and purchase a 500cc Rudge Whitworth for between £50 and £60. There was also the Rudge 'Semi Sports' sidecar and matching two-berth Rudge caravan; the complete outfit was priced at £136.10s. The handbook which came with every motorcycle contained a wealth of information on not only the machine but touring and general road conduct, gradients, countryside features, buildings of interest, ferry services and overseas visits for holidays.

The writer suggested that, once towns were cleared, the motorcyclist should indulge in a bit of speed and 'take advantage of the torrent of power from the engine, bent low over the tank, open the throttle and speed like a black and gold meteorite towards where the road vanishes.' (Black and gold were the standard colours of this Rudge.) Or, 'with the engine pulling smoothly and happily at twelve to fifteen miles per hour, let your eyes and ears and thoughts dwell on the countryside that lies beyond the edge of the road.'

On 27th July 1928 the Bolton Evening News announced that the newly formed Lancashire Dirt Track Racing Association had come to an arrangement with the Bolton Greyhound Racing Co, and dirt track racing was to start at Raikes Lane, Manchester Road, on a shale track inside the existing dog track. The managing director of the Association was Maurice Edwards

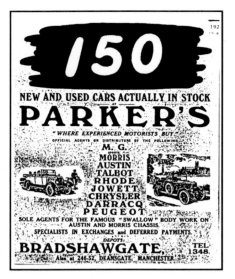

This advert of March 1928 refers to the famous Swallow bodywork. Parker's Bradshawgate site is now covered by the garage and showroom of Williams Motor Company

and his co-director was Albert Horrocks. Competitors in this new sport wore a steel-toed boot which, by either trailing or holding the foot forwards and outwards, allowed the rider to skid round bends at full throttle in a spectacular fashion and with a good chance of showering spectators with dust and shale.

Maurice Edwards was of the opinion that a score or more riders could be found in Bolton 'to take up the skidding art,' and his firm intended building machines for the job.

The inaugural meeting was on 4th August and after a formal opening by Alderman W Rimmer, the 6,000 spectators settled down to a card of eight events, including demonstrations by two experts, Paddy Dean, the 'Australian Thunderbolt', and Ivor Creek of London. One of the prizewinners was a Farnworth man, Jack Smith, who was awarded a silver cup in the 'up to 500cc' Junior Class.

The Bolton Evening News commented, 'It is doubtful if anything interested the crowd more than the side-car events in which the riders and passengers performed some breathless feats of balancing during broadsides.' Most of the machines at this meeting seem to have been fairly standard designs - Sunbeam, Calthorpe, James, Chater-Lea, Douglas, Ariel, Rex Acme, Rudge, Norton and Royal Ruby.

The original MEB in Bark Street, photographed in 1927 with Maurice Edwards at the wheel

The Raikes Park track closed for the winter in October and reopened in March 1929, but the last reported event was in the following April, when Gracie Fields presented the winner with the Golden Helmet. For some reason the track closed soon afterwards and this form of racing disappeared from Bolton.

In 1928 Douglas Hawkes, a well known racing motorist and motor-cyclist of the day, tested the prototype MEB (Maurice Edwards Bolton) three-wheel cyclecar on the Raikes Lane track. Suitably impressed, he took the car, with an air-cooled JAP engine, to the Montlhéry track near Paris and set up new records in the 500cc class: 5 miles at 75.63mph with a flying start and 10 miles at 74.63mph from a standing start. Returning to Bolton, he agreed with Maurice Edwards that other records could be broken and this resulted in a lengthened MEB chassis with a JAP 750cc V-twin engine.

On 23rd December 1928 racing driver Gwenda Stewart, with Douglas Hawkes as passenger, broke four Class J records (750cc cyclecar with passenger) in the modified MEB. They broke four more records on Christmas Day and then, after changing the engine for a 980cc JAP, took another record. (Gwenda and Douglas eventually became man and wife.)

The production models of the MEB appear to have been fitted with the 980cc JAP engine and the sale price was estimated at £105. Just how many were made is not known; it is possible they were produced on a single order basis rather than in a production run. In December 1930 the Light Car and Cyclecar magazine refers to the 'latest models of the MEB cyclecar' and states that an improved body design would be available for 1931. The MEB was produced until at least 1932, because in May 1936 the Helliwell Garage of Marsh Lane, Horwich, was selling a 1932 B/E three-wheeler for £30.

No original MEBs are known to exist today, but a commemorative replica has been designed and constructed as a fundraiser for Bolton Hospice. The chassis material was donated by Edbro plc (successor to Bromilow & Edwards), the excellent mechanical work and bodywork constructed by Jim Marland, former owner of Proteus Cars of Little Lever and the equally high standard of paintwork carried out by the car body makers Coleman-Milne Ltd., Westhoughton. This charitable project was the brainchild of Peter Thurnham, MP for Bolton North West 1983-97, and up to 2004 had helped to raise £20,000 for the Hospice. A good legacy: Peter Thurnham died on 10th May 2008, aged 69.

The mid-1920s saw the birth of the National Safety-First Association, whose efforts were mainly in the direction of road safety. An offshoot of this, the Road Fellowship League, was formed in 1928 and in July, at a meeting of the League in London, the Minister of Transport spoke about the draft Road Traffic Bill, which eventually became the 1930 Road Traffic Act. There were proposals to abolish speed limits and introduce offences such as careless or inconsiderate driving and inconsiderate overtaking. The parking of cars on a corner and giving inefficient hand signals would also come under scrutiny.

Some new Ministry of Transport regulations regarding commercial vehicles, operative from October 1928, were outlined in the Bolton Evening News. All heavy motorcars (between 2 and 5 tons), except those carrying a person at the back who could communicate with the driver, were to carry mirrors. Heavy motor-cars with pneumatic tyres could now travel at 20mph rather than 12mph. The maximum speed of a road locomotive (over 5 tons) towing a trailer was raised from 5mph to 12mph.

In October 1928 Parkers advertised that they were 'The Largest Bolton Firm Handling Austin Cars.' Southerns countered this with 'The Centre of Olympia comes to Bolton,' stating that for the duration of the Olympia Motor Exhibition in London, a special display of Austin models could be viewed in comfort, 'without the distraction of the Motor Show crowds.' The models on show ranged from the Austin Seven tourer at £125 to the Austin Twenty Ranalagh Landaulette at £395.

Kershaws of Moss Bank Way advertised that on the Chevrolet stand at Olympia would be Joseph Kershaw and sales engineer Herman F Barker. The latter was the brother of Trevellyn Barker, who

A photograph of the partially completed MEB replica. The designer and builder, Jim Marland, is on the left and the author on the right

became the Bedford agent in Crook Street. Herman had been a pioneer motorist and, like many, fell foul of the law. In 1903 he was fined 5/- for 'driving at Farnworth in a fast and furious manner, that he did startle a horse and cause it to collide with a lamp post.'

When the Astoria Palais de Danse opened at the corner of Bridge Street and St Georges Road in October 1928, it had a dance floor sprung on wooden cantilevers. Since Bridge Street was on a slope, there was a space beneath the floor which the motor-minded directors made into a garage. It was equipped with a turntable and ducting for exhaust fume extraction and until the onset of the 1939-45 war was leased to John H Bromilow, the local Vauxhall car main agent.

By November 1928 the Clyno agency had been transferred from Southerns to Walter Bradley and Southerns were offering Chrysler De Soto 6-cylinder models from £320, as well as the standard range of Austin vehicles. The association between Southerns and the Morris Commercial agency seems to have ended and, judging by local advertisements, the battle for this agency was now between Pilkingtons, with their showroom at the corner of Deansgate and St Edmund Street, and Parkers.

Walter Bradley, clearly a patriot, advertised in November, 'Bradley's All-British policy for 1929 was decided upon after very careful consideration. They believe that the British car of today is superior to any foreign make, and have selected with great thought what are considered Britain's best productions, including Hillman, Vauxhall, Wolseley, Lea-Francis, Clyno, Singer and Morris.'

Bromilow & Edwards of Bark Street were no longer advertising cars owing to a break up which resulted in Maurice's brothers opening the Springfield Garage in Bradford Street - now part of the trading estate by St Peter's Way. In 1929 John Bromilow and Maurice Edwards parted company, the former continuing with Vauxhall cars from his Bank Street garage and Bridge Street showroom. Maurice was left as sole owner of Bromilow & Edwards Ltd, which then took over the former Foundry Street works of the Chatwood Safe Company and vacated the Bark Street works.

In November 1928 Arnold Kay of Bradshawgate announced that he had acquired 'more commodious premises' in Clive Street (a former Sunday School at the back of the Lido Cinema). He was prepared to 'recondition any car,' as well as provide accommodation for 50 cars in a 'central heated garage'.

A brand new commercial vehicle, the Manchester truck, appeared in Bolton in November. This was a Willys-Overland model by Crossleys of Gorton, available as a 25/30cwt chassis at £245 (complete truck £290) or 30/35cwt chassis at £260 (£305 complete). The agent for Bolton and district was Wilfred Hardman of 1b-3b Bradford Street, which was formerly Percy Heaton's garage. Hardman, who was also the agent for the Overland Whippet saloon, later moved to a purpose-built garage in Hypatia Street, now the BCC Garage.

In May 1927 John Robert Tognarelli, of ice-cream, motor trading and charabanc fame, began a public bus service between Bolton and Manchester, the fare being 1/- single and 1/6d return. He obtained the required licences from the Manchester Watch Committee in August and by 1928 he had nineteen licences from Bolton but only six from Manchester. This meant that thirteen of the buses could carry only 'return' passengers from Manchester, as he was not allowed to collect fares on them. Manchester Corporation wanted control over the revenue from bus passengers in its area.

It was the same with other municipalities with their own bus services, and a co-ordinated scheme was devised, whereby the gross profit of, say, a Salford bus travelling through Manchester went to Manchester Corporation, and vice

Two of J R Tognarelli's long distance coaches, the first one with two doors and a clerestory roof for extra light, access and ventilation

versa. This made things difficult for independent operators with no 'territory' of their own.

When Tognarelli applied for the additional licences in December 1928, the Bolton Evening News reported that he had acquired some land at Poets Corner, near Victoria Station in Manchester, where passengers boarded his buses and he was considering building a bus station and offices at a cost of £45,000. The licences were refused and an appeal to the Ministry of Transport came to nought. He continued to run his buses and battle with the licensing authorities until ill health and continual pressure from the Corporations forced him to give up. His buses, which included Leyland, Associated Daimler and Thornycroft vehicles, were sold to Manchester, Salford, Oldham and Bolton Corporations, and Lancashire United Transport Ltd.

J R Tognarelli continued with vehicle repairs at his Manchester Road garage and in 1931 he was dealing in Commer vehicles. However, by 1935 his name had gone from the directories as a motor trader. He maintained his ice-cream parlour, the Savoy Cafe, over Burtons on Deansgate, serving his customers in the classic Italian garb - black suit, white shirt and apron and black Homburg hat. He retired in 1961 and when he died three years later, after a Requiem Mass at St Patrick's Church, his body was taken back to Italy for interment at Barga Lucca, Tuscany.

The New Year of 1929 opened with an account of Arnold Kay of Bradshawgate being hauled before Bolton magistrates for a couple of motor offences. For allowing his wife and a Charles F Drabble to drive a van without any lights he was fined £1 and the other two 10/- each. He was also fined £1 for permitting machinery to be carried in the van whilst using trade plates. A few weeks later Mr Kay announced he was opening a 'Motoring Academy' in March, to teach driving and how to make running repairs. There would be a special course for youths aged 14 to 17.

The Bolton Journal for 25th January gave approximate figures for the number of licences issued locally in 1928 compared with 1927. In 1928 some 4,400 car licences were issued (4,000 in 1927); 3,500 motorcycle licences (3,400); 2,300 commercial licences (2,200), and 400 hackney licences (380).

Early 1929 saw Southerns continuing to offer De Soto as well as Austins; Edwards Brothers at Springfield announced they were Vulcan agents for Bolton, and 'Yankee Jack' was still on Blackburn Road, now operating as the Autogenous Welding and Car Wrecking Co, selling second-hand spares and offering to buy scrap cars. In March Mr Greenall, who had recently opened a garage at the Wigan Road end of Beaumont Road, advertised the 'Deane showroom, Fernhill' close by, which he had added 'for the benefit of passing trade.' Wilfred Hardman, anxious to promote sales of Willys-Overland cars, advertised the 'National Whippet Week' and in May was offering the Whippet saloon for £198.

In late March 1929 Bolton Corporation took delivery of a new 20hp Austin ambulance which was fitted with 'Hydraulic Lifting Gear for raising to the topmost pair of beds.' 'The Book of Bolton,' published in the same year, states that four motor ambulances were administered by the Fire Brigade Department. The Department had three motorised engines with wheeled escapes and one with an 85-foot turntable ladder, plus a petrol-driven fire pump. The Cleansing Department's fleet included 15 motor wagons, two gully emptiers and a motor sweeping machine. They had about 100 vehicles of various descriptions and 50 horses. The vehicles were more than likely large two-wheeled tipping carts which were used to empty the ashpits of many of the town's terraced houses.

On 16th May 1929 the Bolton Evening News reported a case at Bury magistrates court where some motorcyclists were summonsed for not having efficient brakes. There was a discussion about whether or not those concerned were insured for third party risks, with the Clerk of the Court saying, 'The day will come when all motorists will have to be insured.' Insurance was then a matter of individual preference, but this changed the following year when compulsory insurance was

Bolton's first motor turntable fire engine outside the Swan Hotel, Churchgate. It is a Leyland-Metz. The large searchlight on the left hand side was probably made by Francis Searchlights, Turner Bridge, Bolton

included in the 1930 Road Traffic Act.

By May 1929 Southerns seem to have almost given up selling makes other than Austin. On 4th May they offered 'One only... Chrysler De Soto Saloon.' Three days later they announced that, 'The fruit of our 17 years specialisation (sales and service) of the Austin cars are at the disposal of every Austinist... efficient organisation is here... an Austin repair depot, spares and accessories.' Southerns' apparent disenchantment with American cars appears to have prompted Parkers to advertise that they were the sole district agents for Chrysler 'at Bradshawgate and five branches in Manchester.'

John Bromilow advertised Clyno sports models in his garage beneath the Astoria Palais de Danse, though what unsuspecting buyers thought of him after Clyno went bankrupt later in the year is anyone's guess.

In June 1929 two local lads, Reuben Eckersall (17) and Leslie Tatlock (18), appeared in the County Court after a policeman had caught Eckersall riding a motorcycle on the footpath of Taskers Lane, Kearsley. The motorcycle had no front lamp, no brakes, an inefficient silencer and no petrol tank. The engine was being fed from a small can of petrol. They were fined 17/- each.

On 11th July Walter Bradley of Deansgate advised motorists that he now had models of the Hillman straight-engine variety for £485. This car had been launched at the 1928 Motor Show as Rootes Brothers' answer to the American car for customers at home and abroad who wanted to buy British. Unfortunately the model did not live up to its promised reliability and it suffered a quiet demise.

For Bolton Holiday Week in July 1929, coach operator Arthur Christy offered trips to Gretna Green (18/6d), Harrogate (10/6d), Windermere (10/6d) and Blackpool (5/-). Full board at a Blackpool boarding house could be obtained for 6/6d a day, or bed and breakfast for 4/-.

After the holidays, Southerns were proud to announce that a local

Another Walter Bradley advert for an American car, this time a Knight, sleeve-valved engine driven model, probably a Buick

businessman had been to Devon and Cornwall with four passengers and luggage in an Austin 16 Burnham saloon, covered 1,304 miles over six days and averaged 26mpg with 'no trouble at all'. Parkers' answer to this was a testimonial from an unnamed customer who praised the way the firm had dealt with him, and he had 'never had as good a deal over an old car in his career as a motorist'.

In October 1929 Arnold Kay of Bradshawgate was offering a new model from the Buick stable in the form of the Marquette saloon, priced at £350 to £420, dependent on body. One was offered as a prize in a competition (the conditions were not specified) which he advertised with the following lines:

'To market to market to buy a Marquette,
You've heard all about it but not tried one yet,

So haste you to Bradshawgate and ride out in state,
Then fill in your coupon before you're too late.'

How many Marquettes were actually sold is not known, as Buick decided to withdraw the model in 1931.

There was another promotional event at the Charleston Accumulator Co of 136 St Georges Road. During the 'Great Exide Fortnight' there was the opportunity to win an Essex saloon in a limerick competition, presumably sponsored by Exide. Whether anyone from Bolton won anything is not recorded.

Not to be outdone in the advertising stakes, in October Southerns announced their Austin sales policy. Triplex glass (a sandwich of plate glass and celluloid) and Silentbloc spring shackles (an arrangement whereby components were separated by a rubber sleeve for a quieter ride) were fitted as standard. All models had a chromium finish, there was an 'extended use of aluminium' and two-tone finishes were available in a selection of colours. To emphasise reliability, Southerns stated that the first Austin Twelve was delivered to Bolton 'about seven-and-a-half years ago' and now 'after countless thousands of miles' it was being used as a works car by a well known Bolton firm. It was on the road every day and still able to 'do' Belmont in top gear without lagging.

The inventive mind of Maurice Edwards was revealed once more in a newspaper report of a fire in Bridgeman Street in November 1929. It was during the hours of darkness and the firemen used a portable searchlight designed by Roland Bentley, son of the Chief Fire Officer, and Maurice Edwards. The device comprised a two-wheeled trailer fitted with a petrol-driven generator and two 600 candlepower searchlights; it was intended to be put on the market after the Annual Fire Conference in 1930.

On New Year's Day 1930 Hodges & Knowles, automobile engineers of Kings Hall Buildings, Bradshawgate, announced that they

could supply a 'Traveller's Light Box Van' to the Morris specification, now that Morris Motors themselves were no longer building them. This was the era when commercial travellers carried samples of their firms' products in small vans, specially designed with compartments and drawers for the quick display of their wares to potential customers.

Two days later Fred Snaylam announced he was operating 'Rambler Motor Coaches' and he

had taken over the garage behind the Town Hall recently occupied by W Lees Ltd. At that time he was living in Ulleswater Street, Blackburn Road.

The same issue of the Bolton Evening News mentions a booklet containing sixteen rules issued by the National Safety-First Association which seems to have been a forerunner of the Highway Code. By April 1931 there was another booklet, a 'Highway Code of non-enforceable rules,' this time containing twelve points concerning the safety of the road user.

To make the public aware of this, there was a nationwide competition with a first prize of £1,000 and 600 other prizes ranging from £100 to 10/-. The twelve rules had to be placed in order of importance in four sections - for cyclists, for drivers, for riders and for all road users.

A legal notice in the Bolton Evening News of 1st February 1930 recorded the death of one of Bolton's pioneer motor traders, Isaiah Dootson. He had been living at Birkdale, Southport, and the notice listed his business interests. Besides the motor enterprises at Bridgeman Place and St Georges Road, which he called the International Motor Co, he owned a depot with the same name at White City, one of the centres of

One of many Bolton motor traders advertising in the mid-1920s

Manchester's motor world. There was another business based at Bridgeman Place, the Bolton Tanning Co, and he owned the Argus Manufacturing Co in Southport. The Bolton directory for 1927 also lists 158-160 Crook Street (later Trev Barker's) as one of his depots.

For a number of years 116 Bradshawgate had been Albert Horrocks' motor establishment, then by February 1930 it had become a motorcycle depot with the rather odd title, Deansgate Motor Mart Ltd. The manager was Alec Jackson, a former TT and Grand Prix rider. Later in the month the firm announced that they were the sole agents for the Triumph Super Seven small car. This was produced between 1927 and 1932 in seven different body styles; the Bolton dealer does not appear to have survived beyond the latter date.

In March 1930 'Bolton's First Gigantic Motor Auction', held in the Bark Street building formerly occupied by Bromilow & Edwards, was attended by a crowd of about 300, including many local motor traders. The Bolton Evening News reported that high-powered cars were not in great demand, but the smaller cars sold well. A 1926 Clyno went for 30 guineas, a 1927 Salmson for 38 guineas and a 1926 Austin Seven for 44 guineas. (The pricing of cars in guineas was fairly standard practice at auctions at that time.) The name of the auctioneers was given as Bolton Car Auctions and according to the paper, the event was 'what's been wanted in Bolton for a long time'.

Bolton garages advertising at this time included John Fletcher's Church House Garage, which had the Swift cars agency. Unfortunately for purchasers, the make did not survive 1931. Star Auto Engineers of Endon Street, Chorley Old Road, claimed to be the 'Most Progressive and up-to-date Garage in Bolton', and whilst they had only been in business three years, they had 300 satisfied customers. They were agents for Essex cars, an American model which disappeared in 1932.

This period saw the gradual changeover from high to low pressure car tyres and to encourage this Thistlethwaites of Burns Street offered free replacement wheels. The old high pressure 'clincher' type of wheel rim could not accommodate the softer walls of the low pressure covers.

Yankee Jack was still advertising welding and car breaking, while the Angle Bank Welding Co of Rishton Lane, Great Lever, seemed to be after his business, claiming, 'We can weld anything from a traction engine to a tooth in a watch.' Harry Woodall had taken over the garage on High Street from Hennessey's and continued to offer to repair motor hoods, although this style of coachwork was becoming dated, except for sports cars. John H Bromilow had various cars for hire, either self-drive or with a driver, from his premises under the Astoria Palais de Danse. Motorists could garage their cars there for 2/6d (daytime) or 3/6d (day and night), and a wash and polish could be had for 2/6d.

In July Southerns advertised the 'New and Bigger' Austin Seven saloon with 'pneumatic upholstery' (air pressurised cushions) at £140.

The model would seat four adults in somewhat cramped, but cosy, comfort. It was also stated that the car had improved brakes, which in effect meant that the front and rear brakes were coupled together. Prior to this, the foot-pedal operated only the rear brakes of the Austin Seven and the handbrake worked those at the front.

The 1930 Road Traffic Act received Royal Assent on 1st August. It laid down a wide range of regulations for motorists and motorcyclists, such as having at least third party insurance and a minimum age of 16 for motorcyclists. The Act did not introduce the official testing of drivers, and the abolition of speed limits for cars and motorcycles would not be implemented until after further consultation with local authorities. As for commercial vehicles, until 1929 these were governed by the 1903 Heavy Locomotive Act which decreed a limit of 12mph. This was increased to 20mph for pneumatic tyred vehicles in that year, then 30mph in 1931.

Some 58 offences were created. Driving without a licence or employing an unlicensed driver incurred a maximum fine of £20 for

Bradshawgate, near the junction with Deansgate, photographed about 1929. A Sunbeam tourer drives ahead of a Leyland coach and Morris Oxford, Austin and Rover cars

the first offence; £50 or 3 months for the second. Reckless or dangerous driving meant a £50 fine or 4 months; £100 or 4 months for the second offence, plus possible disqualification for a period decided by the court. Promoting or taking part in a race or speed trial on public roads: £50 or 3 months plus 12 months disqualification. Failure to stop after an accident, give name and address and report to a police station: £20 first offence; £50 second or 3 months. Driving a vehicle without the owner's consent: £50 or 3 months; £100 second and/or 12 months, at the court's discretion. Driving, or attempting to drive under the influence of drink or drugs: £50 or 4 months; £100 second, and/or 4 months, or 6 months and/or a fine at the court's discretion.

Until 1930, passenger vehicles were licensed by local authorities using powers initiated by an Act of 1847 to regulate horse-drawn carriages. The operation of public service vehicles was, according to the Minister of Transport, 'an impossible state of affairs which must be cleaned up', and resulted in the creation of Traffic Commissioners and Traffic Areas, route licensing, Road Service Licences on stage and express carriages, Certificates of Fitness and a requirement for buses carrying more than twenty passengers to have a conductor. Some of Bolton's small businesses were no doubt thankful for new specifications

under the Act. For example, from October 1930 motorcycles had to be fitted with rear number plates measuring eight inches by six inches, instead of four or five inches square.

In November 1930 Walter Bradley, Chairman of the Corporation Transport Committee, went with other officials to Leeds and to London to inspect diesel engined buses. Diesel fuel was then retailing at 1/2d a gallon, as opposed to petrol at 1/- a gallon, and the Leeds bus averaged 12.8mpg. It was Bradley's considered opinion that the petrol engines in Bolton's buses could be changed for diesel ones without too much trouble.

From December, all buses and charabancs which had used Victoria Square as their terminus were relocated to Moor Lane. Arthur Christy objected and wrote to the Council to say that Victoria Square was centrally located and ideal. He thought the recently-erected war memorial in Victoria Square was in the wrong place and passengers should not be made to suffer because of the 'short-sightedness of those responsible for the siting of the Cenotaph'. The charabanc operators were allowed a week's grace to complete their arrangements at the new and somewhat stark bus station.

The first local case of 'driving under the influence' was reported on 15th

December. The culprit was Alexander Rea of 76 Crosby Road, who was seen driving from one side of Bradshawgate to the other.

PC Aspinall tried to apprehend him, but for some reason Mr Rea managed to reach the Central Police Station, where it was noticed that he was under the influence of drink. He then staggered back to his car and drove via the pavement on to Deansgate, where he was stopped by a police motor patrol. He was fined £5, had his licence suspended for 12 months and incurred witness costs of £2.1.6d.

The year 1930 ended with rumblings of financial discontent in the business world. It was a time when the motor trade, which until then had catered mainly for the fairly well-heeled, had to look to a wider range of customers, particularly those who would be content with lower priced and lower powered cars. Manufacturers would have to invest in mass-production of a wider range of models and some amalgamations would be inevitable.

This eventually resulted in the motor trade being dominated by the 'Big Five' of Ford, Vauxhall, Austin, Morris and Rootes. Their main output in the 1930s was in the 7-12hp category, together with sports tourers for customers who were not directly affected by the Depression.

There had been a big change in the volume of traffic in just a few years: here, just one taxi emerging from the canopy of the former Trinity Street Railway Station in the mid-1920s is surrounded by returning holidaymakers

General Expansion 1931-1938

The New Year of 1931 dawned with thick fog blanketing Manchester Road, resulting in an eight-vehicle collision under the Burnden railway bridge. A few days later the Bolton Evening News reported a speech by the Minister of Transport, defending the abolition of speed limits for cars: 'If a speed limit had been fixed it would have been very difficult to enforce. It was hoped that at all times motorists would drive in a responsible manner.' He also said that from 1st February the hours for drivers of public service and commercial vehicles would be limited. Presumably he felt the combination of these three matters would make for generally safer motoring.

The legal requirement for insurance under the 1930 Act was noted by Messrs Cleary & Marshall of 29a Newport Street, who advertised 'Motor Insurance on the Instalment System' on 5th January. Perhaps John Hodkin of 9 John Cross Street went to see them after being the first person to be convicted in Bolton for driving without insurance.

At the end of January two more cases which concerned the new Road Traffic Act were reported. Arthur Roberts of 'Briarfield', Blackburn Road, was fined 10/- for riding a motorcycle without a pillion seat; he was on the petrol tank and his lady friend was on the saddle. Three youths from Wigan, who appeared in court for hanging on to the tailboard of a lorry going through Westhoughton, had their case dismissed with a warning that future offenders would not be treated leniently.

Bolton's first traffic lights were installed in January 1931, at the junction of Bradshawgate and Great Moor Street. A year later the Chief Constable recommended thirteen more sets for the borough, mainly in the town itself.

Advertisers at the beginning of the year included Walter Pilling of Great Moor Street, who offered a Citroen at £265, and Reilly &

Brookes, also of Great Moor Street, who had a two-hour battery repair service. They would also overhaul a magneto, dynamo or starter in three hours. Richard Pilkington had moved into the former premises of Hardman & Jacques, Garside Street, and Walter Pilling was using his depot in Hugo Street/Turk Street for the new process of cellulose repainting.

At the start of 1931 there were a million licensed cars in Britain and, according to the Autocar buyer's guide, 261 different models were available. 49.44% of these were from British firms, 20.5% were American, 17.1% French, 6.5% Italian, 3.25% Belgian, 2.5% German and 2.15% Austrian. This year saw the opening of the Ford works at Dagenham and the decision by General Motors to build a British version of the Chevrolet truck. A new production line was set up at Luton, Bedfordshire, and the first Bedford truck emerged as a two-tonner, almost identical to the Chevrolet. The establishment of these two major manufacturing facilities contributed to the reduced level of unemployment in the south of the country, but had a minimal impact on the developing recession in the mining, textile and heavy engineering industries of the north.

Local motor traders continued to offer their wares and services. A hand tipping lorry (probably a Ford) could be purchased from Gordons for £227, or in hydraulic form for £270. John H Bromilow, Vauxhall main agent, offered his services from his depot in Bank Street and showroom at 46 Bridge Street. He also had second-hand cars for sale in the Astoria garage opposite. Entwistle & Walker of Derby Street would rebore and fit new pistons and rings to four-cylinder engines such as Morris and Austin for £10, and Thistlethwaite's tyre depot was giving a free map and mileage chart with every purchase until the Whitsun holiday.

An ominous sign of the economic state came in April, when Wilfred Hardman reduced the prices of his Manchester truck range. The 30/35cwt model was down from £260 to £230 and the dropside truck from £305 to £275. In the same month, Walter Bradley, hoping for good sales of the new Hillman Wizard, had an unveiling ceremony by the Mayor, Alderman Warburton (of baking fame). It was not a very successful car and soon disappeared.

A mid-1930s Bedford, short wheelbase truck outside Barker's Crook Street showrooms. Note the trade plate 072BN used by Barkers

Competition for repairs was becoming keen. Ross Isherwood, who had moved from the small garage in Shipgates to the Breightmet Garage on Bury Road, offered to decarbonise a standard car for 25/-, supply Morris Cowley axle shafts for 10/- each, crown wheel and pinion sets for £2.17.6d and cylinder head gaskets for 1/9d each. John Fletcher of the Church House Garage, Churchgate, stressed the quality of his mechanics: 'Special staff employed to deal exclusively with electrical work, also for mechanical matters... no apprentices to tinker with your car.'

Despite the impending financial crisis, Bolton's motor coach trade seemed to fare reasonably well. Arthur Binns had offices at the corner of Bark Street and Knowsley Street; Fred Snaylam ran his services from Newport Street and Arthur Christy from Moor Lane. Fred Lomax (Ivanhoe Motors) of Saville Street offered a trip to Cartmel Races on Whit Monday for 10/- return; William Knowles would take you to Blackpool for 5/- return, Morecambe for 6/-, Windermere and Keswick for 13/6d or Matlock for 10/-.

When the new Road Traffic Act regulations for coach operators reached Bolton firms, they were met with 'irritation and indignation' according to a Bolton Evening News report on 11th May. Detailed returns and forms had to be completed, involving 'hours and hours of intensive clerical work'. Arthur Christy complained, 'We will have extra expense, and there will be a fight against objections to the running of many services. We want fair play for motor-coach owners... Why not encourage this young and thriving industry, at the present time there is more demand than ever for cheap travel... The public will be the biggest losers in the long run if railways and bus concerns crush the coach owners.' Mr Christy said the man with one or two coaches would not be able to afford the additional fees and legal costs involved in licence applications and possible litigation disputes.

When applying for road service licences, full particulars had to be given in triplicate: road numbers, times, halts, mileage and time of year. Mr Christy said he had already submitted eleven applications for the Northern area, nine for Yorkshire, eight for the West Midlands, seven for the East Midlands, five for South Scotland, two for the South and one each for the Western, Eastern, Metropolitan and South Wales areas. Similar applications would have been in process with other tour operators. The coaches could not run without applications being granted, so this imposed restrictions on the firms' ability to advertise in advance. No doubt many chances were taken in this respect and the operators managed to balance the legal requirements with public demand.

Self-contained motoring holidays were popular at this time and if a tent and Primus stove were just a bit too primitive, there was the motorised caravan, or one that could be towed. In June 1931 the Bolton Evening News carried advertisements for three local firms: the Northern Caravan Co of 1 Fold Street offered a car trailer caravan for hire; Smith's Garage at Tottington went a bit further and offered both motor and caravan, and

Messrs Holding of Hanover Street, auto engineers and coachbuilders, would sell you a model to suit your requirements. The situation was not lost on Maurice Edwards and about this time Bromilow & Edwards designed and manufactured a neat and compact folding caravan, the Collapsivan, for towing by a two-seater sports car.

On 22nd June 1931 Kershaws advertised Chevrolet and Bedford models. This was the last time the firm had any official connection with the Chevrolet commercial range and probably the only time they had anything to do with the newcomer to the British commercial vehicle world, for on 26th June the Bolton Evening News carried the first advertisement for Trev Barker's motor garage at 158-160 Crook Street, sole distributors for Chevrolet and Bedford vehicles.

This firm had its roots in Darwen, where in the 1920s Charles Trevellyn Barker had a garage working on both private and commercial vehicles, with a leaning towards American models such as Chevrolet and Oakland. Aware of the load-carrying advantages of six-wheel lorries such as Leyland and

An early 1930s Bedford WLB 20-seater coach popular with the small operator. At least one, known as 'The Rocket', ran between the Royal Oak and Harwood during the 1930s

Thornycroft, he designed a six-wheel vehicle based on the four-wheel Chevrolet chassis. This followed the usual practice of fitting a trailing, undriven rear axle. Conversion to double rear axle drive was expensive, particularly since the basic idea was to increase carrying capacity rather than traction.

Trev Barker also produced an articulated model, one of which was sold to Lever's Haulage of Farnworth, who later became the Vauxhall/Bedford main agents in the town. Another was sold to Barlow Brothers, general carriers of Farnworth. In August 1930 he registered a design for a semi-forward control van, and a version of this appeared as a six-wheeler.

Most cars of this period had radiator grilles, front and rear bumpers, door handles, wiper arms and blades made shiny with either chrome or nickel plating. On expensive cars there was a certain amount of silver plating. In some cases, exposed brackets were stove enamelled (a heated paint process) to protect them from the elements. To cater for the refurbishment of such items, in August 1931 Walter Pilling of Great Moor Street advertised sterling and nickel plating, plus stove enamelling. He grandly stated that he could tackle anything from a spoon to a motor car without a problem.

The requirements of the law regarding drivers' licences caused a bit of trouble from time to time in 1931. In August a man was fined £1 because his licence was out of date. He had not been notified about renewal and the Bolton Evening News thought this was wrong in view of the fact that holders of dog licences were sent renewal notices.

The Bolton Evening News of 3rd September 1931 advertised the sale of a motor coach and carrying business, complete with centrally heated garage and petrol pumps, all in working order and insured, and with plenty of land 'for opening out.' The seller was Mrs Annie Copple of 4 Osborne Grove. Mrs Copple may have been retiring from the business, or perhaps it was the worsening financial situation. A few days later the Chancellor presented an emergency Budget. Petrol went up 2d a gallon; the standard rate of Income Tax went up by 6d to 5/- in the pound; 1d went on the price of a pint of beer, and there were cuts in public spending, teachers' and policemen's pay and unemployment benefit.

Despite the fiscal gloom and doom, the local motor traders continued their optimistic advertising.

Bromilow & Edwards, having more or less ceased retailing cars, branched out into the coach body business. The Bolton Evening News of 2nd October reported that the Mayor, Alderman Warburton, had inspected a 29-seater Pullman deluxe model made for Yelloway Motor Services of Rochdale.

On 15th October there was a full-page advertisement to coincide with the London Motor Show. John H Bromilow of Bridge Street offered the new Vauxhall Cadet saloon for £285 with a 17hp engine or £485 with the larger 'Silent Six' 24hp engine. The Cadet was the first major fruit of the General Motors/Vauxhall merger and was the first British car to have a synchromesh gearbox to make driving easier.

The Bolton Motor Company, Wilfred Hardman, Gordons, Bradleys and Arnold Kay between them offered Standard, Fiat, Willys, Ford, Daimler, Wolseley, Hillman, Singer, Jowett, Buick, Armstrong-Siddeley and Crossley. Southerns had the full range of Austin cars, large and small.

The normal control Chevrolet articulated wagon which Barker's sold to Lever's Haulage. Note the late 1920s Bolton registration WH1414

Parkers announced they were the 'Olympia of the North' and no doubt they were awaiting delivery of a new car by William Lyons of Swallow coachwork fame, known simply as the SS 1. The model became known in some quarters as 'the cad's car,' as many people later associated it with some of the more dubious second-hand car dealers and devotees of dog racing. It had a rather long bonnet housing a six-cylinder Standard engine and the driver's legs, a low-slung body and cramped coupé seating at the end of the chassis. Its appearance suggested a price tag of £1,000, but it cost only £310. Advertisements claimed that the 'delightful lines' were a joy to behold, and the car had 'flashing acceleration' to 75mph. It was the first of a range of SS and Jaguar sports cars and saloons of distinctive design which were sold by Parkers until the firm closed.

In October 1931 Arnold Kay advertised the Croft Commercial Car, a battery-powered tricycle aimed at easing delivery costs for milkmen, fruit and vegetable vendors and shop-to-shop distributors of bakery products. It came in two models: 3-5cwt for £69.10s and 7-10cwt for £75; road tax was £4 and estimated running costs were 1d per mile. Arnold Kay advertised it only once, so it would appear that not many local traders took advantage of the offer. Perhaps they were put off by having to buy charging equipment and the limited range of 25-30 miles. It was not until the mid-1930s that electric vehicles became popular, and then only with large concerns such as the Co-op and milk retailers.

A more suitable vehicle for the local delivery market was the Raleigh three-wheeler, advertised by the Starcliffe Motor & Engineering Company of Moses Gate in November 1931. Known as the Safety Seven, it had a 5cwt capacity and cost £75. Unlike the Croft, which had its single wheel at the rear, the Raleigh had the single wheel at the front, making a van body more feasible. It was powered by an air-cooled V-twin engine, was capable of 50-55mph, had a three-speed gearbox with reverse and was steered by motorcycle-type handlebars. The rights to this van were purchased by a former Raleigh designer, Tom Williams, in 1934 and the following year it emerged as the Reliant van. It survived, with an Austin Seven engine, until the 1950s and the Reliant firm is still in existence today.

In 1931 Arthur Fox opened a new garage at the Bury Road end of the recently completed Crompton Way. This garage closed in 2000, when it was owned by Bolton and Cooper, but was reopened as the Bolton Motor Company on 1st November 2002 by Mr C Brooks and Mr D Brabin.

In December 1931 William Knowles, who dealt in Morris Commercial vehicles, advertised the North End Garage at Astley Bridge. He also asked the public to view the 'All British' vehicles on display at his Newport Street garage, formerly the premises of Auto & Engineering Ltd.

In March 1932 The Bolton Motor Co invited motorists to inspect the 15/18hp Lanchester 'with Fluid Flywheel,' a hydraulic mechanism which eventually developed into today's automatic transmission. This Lanchester would have been an expensive car to tax, as it had a 2.5 litre, six-cylinder engine, and it was not too economical on fuel. The AJS saloon with a 9hp engine, advertised by Wilfred Hardman, would perhaps have had a better chance of success. The AJS firm had been taken over by Willys-Overland-Crossley in 1931, but it disappeared two years later.

By March 1932 Joseph Kershaw, the former Chevrolet dealer, had given up the Moss Bank Way premises and had taken over the dealership for Commer goods and passenger vehicles from J R Tognarelli at 115-117 Manchester Road. Among other firms advertising at this time was the Endon Street Garage, offering a 'Day and Night Service.' They would carry out 'repairs whilst you sleep', although whether the local residents got any sleep is debatable. In a terse announcement on 29th March, 'Edge, the Coachpainter' of Lever Street promised 'Old cars made new at reasonable cost' - the equivalent of today's 'quick flash-over'.

An optimistic attitude in Bolton's motor trade can be seen in three contrasting advertisements in early April. A vendor hoping to make his way under the title Motor Spares and Mart of Great Moor Street had for sale 'Two Ford Lorries - Cheap.' Further up the scale, Messrs Brockbank & Baxter opened a new garage at the junction of Crompton Way and Blackburn Road (now the Lidl supermarket site). The third advertisement was for Fred Snaylam's brand new Leyland coach (WH3787), which had a special heating device and 'automatic control of the inner temperature'. Passengers would have a warm and comfortable journey in winter, perhaps to Blackpool illuminations and the odd public house on the return run.

Trev Barker invited customers to inspect Chevrolet and Bedford trucks at Crook Street between 4th and 9th April, and 'as a gesture of goodwill sumps will be refilled free

The SS sports car, designed by William Lyons, which was the sensation of the 1930 Motor Show in London

with Speedwell oil.' The following week he had the latest range of Bedfords on display. The 16.9hp light delivery chassis was £135; with a van on the chassis £168. The 27hp, 30cwt chassis was £175; with lorry £210; tipper £226; box van £230. Short two-ton chassis £198; lorry £236. Long two-ton chassis £210; lorry £250. There were also chassis for bus body fitting in 14 and 20 seat versions.

Advertising the latest Cadet family saloon, J H Bromilow stated, 'Even a child can drive the New Vauxhall Cadet,' which was a somewhat dangerous thing to say, even in those days. Later in the month, Mr Bromilow took a slightly different view of the Cadet. It was 'A truly Aristocratic Car at Democratic Prices.'

Parker's advertisements continued to suggest the firm was the principal motor trader in Bolton. In April they announced that they were agents for Morris, Ford, Austin, Standard and Rover cars. The claims would be countered by a main dealer, such as the Bolton Motor Co, who on 16th April stated they were main agents for Standard and Humber cars and that their staff were specially trained on those vehicles.

Accounts of two fires drew attention to the hazards surrounding motor repairs. One was at the Star Auto Engineering's Endon Street Garage in April. It was caused by an

electrical short circuit 'on a car being cleaned with petrol' and the staff of five managed to put it out. The second fire was in May in a row of six garages owned by Ross Isherwood on Bury Road, Breightmet.

As the holiday season approached, the Bolton Evening News offered its readers a free motor route guide, containing fifty routes to country and seaside destinations with distances from Bolton. If a motorist felt that his car needed a check over, he was advised to visit Tognarelli's new garage on Manchester Road (the site of Lythgoe Motors). He claimed he had the 'Largest and Most Modern Solid and Pneumatic Tyre Depot in the North,' and motorists could expect first class repairs, as he only employed experienced mechanics.

On 24th June the Bolton Evening News published a photograph of

holidaymakers boarding one of Arthur Christy's coaches for Blackpool. With them was Alice Pennington, Bolton's contestant for the title of Cotton Queen. The cost of holiday coach travel can be seen in the 1st July advertisements. For 15/- you could go to North Wales with Fred Snaylam, or Gretna Green with Arthur Christy.

Motorists resident in the Bury Road/Crompton Way district had their choice of garage increased in July 1932 with the opening of Park Garage, 499 Bury Road, by Ted Beardsworth. He advertised that he was a practical engineer with 18 years' experience and was a specialist in decarbonising, at an average cost of 4/- per cylinder. This involved the removal of carbon from the piston crown and round the valves, and for a 10hp Ford, Austin or Morris, it had to be done every 2,000-3,000 miles. Examples of engine overhaul costs at that time can be seen in Pilkington's advertisements. An engine rebore and fitting oversize pistons on a Morris Oxford, Ford or Austin 12 cost £8; for a Hillman 14 it was £9, and for a six-cylinder Austin or Essex, £13.10s.

The small print of the 1930 Road Traffic Act was responsible for court cases from time to time. The Bolton Evening News of 18th July 1932 reported the first prosecution in Bolton concerning regulations for garages and their petrol pumps. Henry Nuttall & Son of Farnworth were ordered to pay the costs of the case against them for not having their pumps stamped by the Weights & Measures Department, to ensure the correct amounts were dispensed. Ignorance of the regulations was not accepted as a defence.

In August 1932, sixteen-year-old Stanley Armitage of Bath Street was fined 4/- for failing to notify the change of ownership of a motorcycle he had sold to a friend, Harold Taylor (19). This came to light after an accident at Smithills. After wartime service in the RAF, Stanley Armitage ran a small garage in Dawson Lane, off Chorley Old Road.

In mid-September 1932 the motorist was faced with an increase of 3d per gallon of petrol. Local firms and Bolton Corporation were quite concerned about the increase to their fuel bills and coach proprietor Arthur Christy said it would cost him another £600 per year. The next month the Corporation experimented with a Leyland double-deck bus fitted with a diesel engine. The week's trial on the Townleys route did not quite meet with the approval of Mr Barnard, the Transport Manager, who complained about the smell of the fuel, the black smoke when starting up, and the fact that diesel engines wear out more quickly than petrol engines. Despite this, the Corporation changed to diesel engines and by 1940, in a bus fleet of 214 vehicles, only 9 had petrol engines.

On 26th September the Bolton Evening News reported on a visit to an open-air car mart in Great Moor Street (believed to be the site of the Labour Exchange). The unnamed proprietor said that most of his trade was done in accident damaged cars and they were in 'various states of wear and tear.' Prices ranged from £5 to £10 each. Little more is known of this 'old banger' firm, so it would seem to have been short lived.

To coincide with the London Motor Show in October, the Bolton Evening News had a page of advertisements from the main dealers and agents. J H Bromilow offered the new Vauxhall Cadet and Gordons of Higher Bridge Street had the new product from Dagenham, the 8hp Ford Model Y at £120, aimed at the mass market. Walter Bradley had Hillman, Wolseley, Singer and Jowett; Arnold Kay the Manchester-made Crossley, and Parkers announced they were the Northern distributors for the more expensive Lagonda sports car.

Towards the end of 1932, the Coventry Reboring and Welding Co of 37a Blackburn Road (Yankee Jack Bennett's address) offered to overhaul engines and fit oversize pistons, and rebuild and re-cut worn valve seatings. The work would be done by 'Coventry Experts' and the correct alloys were 'chosen by metallurgists'.

In January 1933 the increasing number of cars in Bolton prompted the Evening News to raise the question of parking in the town centre. A reporter had counted 15 cars parked on Bradshawgate between Deansgate and Great Moor Street and asked, 'How long is it to be allowed to continue?' At that time there was free parking for just 23 cars; 12 on Nelson Square and 11 on the south side of Victoria Square. There was also parking on Moor Lane, for which a charge was made.

On 31st January 1933 the Bolton Evening News wireless reporter described a journey in a car owned by Mr R W Proffitt of Knowsley Street, wireless and electrical goods dealer. It was fitted with a Transitone receiver, designed for use in private and public vehicles by the Philadelphia Storage Battery Co

Traffic on Deansgate in the mid-1930s, showing the wide variety of makes available by then. Identifiable on the right hand side are, from right to left, a Bean tourer, a Hillman Minx, an Alvis and a Standard. The two in the foreground on the left are an Austin 7 tourer and a Morris 8 saloon

(Philco), and costing 33 guineas. Reception was perfect, even at 50mph, and there was no interference from the car ignition system. The set fitted neatly under the scuttle, with the control panel on the dashboard; speakers were concealed in the bodywork and the aerial was a sheet of copper gauze under the roof lining. The reporter looked forward to the day when every 'good-class' car or motorcycle would be fitted with such an accessory.

Under the heading 'Dangers of the Road,' in February 1933 the Bolton Evening News published accident statistics for the previous year. 687 persons had been injured in traffic accidents in Bolton and worse, 24 had been killed. There had been 1,997 accidents, an increase of 343 over 1931. The apparent causes were: carelessness by pedestrians 331; skidding 173; defective brakes and engine trouble 46; miscellaneous unknown causes 941; carelessness by cyclists 132; carelessness by motorists 374.

There was another fire at Star Auto Engineering's Endon Street Garage in February 1933, this time causing some £300 worth of damage. Work resumed two days later using new equipment in adjacent premises, so the firm does not seem to have suffered greatly. However it must have upset proprietor James Jackson a bit, for two weeks later he was fined for assaulting a Robert Pringle outside a Bolton hotel.

What seems to have been the first Bolton advertisement for antifreeze appeared in 1933. This was 'No Freeze' from Moscrop's Lion Oil Works. Many motorists did not trust antifreeze, as some types had a corrosive effect on radiator cores, and instead they would drain off the water every winter night, or put a small, shallow paraffin heater under the engine. Moscrop's also advertised an upper cylinder lubricant called 'Upcyllub.' This was added to petrol when filling up, in proportions based on so many eggcup-fulls per gallon. Its function was to reduce the build-up of hard carbon on the piston crown, combustion chamber and valve

stems, which led to pre-ignition 'pinking'; 'running on' when the ignition was switched off, and valves sticking in the guides.

A Parkers advertisement in February 1933 gives some idea of the costs involved in purchasing, insuring and taxing a small car. Their quote for a new Austin Seven was £125 for the car, £8 for full insurance and £2.4s for a quarter's tax. Payment by instalments would be arranged, with a deposit of £35.4s (cash or exchange).

The £8 'full insurance' was what is today known as fully comprehensive. A few months later, F Hulme, an insurance agent of 24 Moorside Avenue, Doffcocker, advertised his rates for motorists. Three months' third party for an 8hp car was £1; 12hp £1.7.6d; 15hp £1.15s. All less 10% if only owner-driven. He also offered insurance for motorcycles: a 350cc machine was 10/- and 550cc was 11/6d.

The car battery of the day was not as reliable as the modern equivalent. It suffered damage due to harsh road springs and road surfaces of setts. The practice of topping-up the electrolyte with tap water, together with forgetting to check the level of the battery, led to plates warping and shorting-out. These and other problems meant work for Bolton's battery repairers. Vickers of 73/75 Newport Street were 'Battery Builders and Specialist in Auto

Electrics' and Stonehills of 100 Bradshawgate were 'Sole Official Agent for Lucas, CAV and Rotax Batteries'. The Charleston Accumulator Co of 136 St Georges Road had '30 years Battery Experience'; this firm was owned by the Lorenzelli family until it closed in the 1960s.

In the run up to the 1933 Bolton holiday week, rail and coach operators competed for business. 128 special trains would run during the week, 40 of them to Blackpool, and some 200 coaches would leave Bolton over the weekend. A Third Class return train ticket to Blackpool was 5/6d; London was £1.12.9d; and Windermere 12/-. For the more affluent, Thomas Cook offered a 16-day, all-in trip to Ireland for £4.15s, a holiday in Switzerland for £14.0.6d, and 13-day cruises from Liverpool to Lisbon, Madeira, Casablanca and Vigo for 15 guineas. For the less affluent, there was 'Ramsden's Special Cycle Run' to Ribchester on 11th June, with a free cup of tea thrown in.

The motorist who felt that his car carpet was not up to standard for a holiday could contact Horrockses of Ridgway Gates, who advertised carpets carefully shaped to fit round levers and pedals - 'Bring a paper pattern or an old carpet for a quotation.' Holidaymakers who wanted their luggage taken to, and collected from, their hotels could use a local carrier such as H Marsh

Thomas Relph was among many taxi proprietors who had expanded their business since the 1920s. Now motor cars were in demand for funerals as well as weddings

of St Germain Street, Farnworth, who offered carriage to Rhyl for 3/- per case.

The Bolton motorist who wanted to take his holiday in a new car had a reasonable choice. Southerns had the Austin Seven in its latest form, with a wheelbase extended by six inches to give a little more legroom. The slightly larger Austin Ten could be bought in standard saloon form or with a sliding roof, or even as an open tourer. Walter Bradley offered the Hillman Minx, a car fitted with Bendix brakes, which gave trouble if not set up correctly.

The motorist who bought a new car for the holidays would have done so a few weeks in advance so that the engine could be 'run in' in the approved manner: not exceeding 30mph, operating the accelerator pedal gently for the first 500-1,000 miles and oil changes at 500 miles and then every 2,000 miles. It was the practice to stick a notice on the rear window announcing, 'Running-In. Please Pass.'

A 'Safety Week' in June 1933 suggested that it would be a good idea for all drivers to take a test (legislation at that time only covered PSV and taxi drivers) and to instruct children in road safety. The Police Department gave lessons in conduct at traffic lights and the Bolton Evening News of 21st June carried a photograph of Inspector Gledhill at the Blackburn Road/Crompton Way crossing.

One of Bolton's pioneer motor engineers, Joseph Kershaw, died in August at the age of 65. He had been in the motor haulage business for over twenty years and before that owned Sheep House and Harricroft farms in Smithills. He had been a Council member of the Royal Lancashire Agricultural Society and his home was at 1175 Chorley Old Road. His garage business on Manchester Road was taken over by W H Kershaw.

Two more small garages advertised for the first time in the summer of 1933 - the Bridgefoot Garage on Chorley Street and a service station in Lucy Street, Whitecroft Road, owned by George Marsh.

In August the Transport Department took delivery of an experimental AEC double-deck bus called the Q bus. It was fitted with a 7.4 litre petrol engine and the coachwork was very advanced, with a rounded enclosed front, a tramcar-style lifesaver, and a front entrance door. The bus lasted for six or seven months before being sold, via William Knowles Ltd, to Yeoman's Motors of Hereford.

The Q was the only non-Leyland bus purchased by Bolton Corporation between 1908 and 1946. In 1933 they acquired five Leyland Titan double-deckers with bodywork by Bromilow & Edwards, who had started making bus bodies the previous year. A few months later the firm was re-formed as a public company.

Bolton's principal dealers advertised their wares in October to coincide with the London Motor Show. Aiming at a wide clientele, Walter Bradley had models ranging from the stately Daimler to the two-cylinder Jowett. Entwistle & Walker offered Hillman, Talbot, Triumph and Standard, and they were also agents for a new commercial vehicle called the Surrey-Dodge, in 30cwt and two-ton capacity. This was an American truck made by Dodge Brothers (GB) at Kew, Surrey, and was in competition with the Guy Wolf two-tonner offered by Wilfred Hardman.

Towards the end of 1933 the growing toll of road deaths and injuries was a source of mounting concern for national and local bodies. In November Mr Rhys Davies, MP for Westhoughton, addressed the Pedestrian Association in Manchester and appealed for stronger such associations so that views could be expressed in Parliament 'and adequate measures taken to stop the slaughter'.

In the same month there was a meeting between the Home Office and the National Union of Teachers, at which the union had declined to have its members used as 'traffic controllers' outside schools in order to free 'hundreds of constables' for other duties. The NUT said it would be unfair to drivers and parents and 'impose a strain on women teachers which they might be unable to stand'. It was pointed out by the Bolton Evening News that Bolton teachers were always willing to stand at crossings if there were no policemen nearby.

The bodies for these two double-decker buses were made by Bromilow & Edwards for Bolton Corporation in the mid-1930s. The photograph was taken on Deansgate, close to Whitaker's Emporium

At the beginning of December the Bolton Evening News reported that Inspector Gledhill had been appointed by the Chief Constable to visit every Bolton school and deliver lectures on road safety. Leaflets were distributed and posters were displayed near schools. The Chief Constable also authorised the provision of specially marked pedestrian crossings at twelve points in the town, to be indicated by white lines, and 'if their usefulness is confirmed then they will have permanent signs erected near them.'

New licences for commercial carriers, due to come into force in 1934, were discussed in the Bolton Evening News in December. The Public Carrier's Licence for the haulage contractor carrying goods for hire or reward would cost £1.10s and last for two years. The Limited Carrier's Licence was for those who carried goods in connection with their business and carried certain items for hire or reward linked with the business. It would cost £1 and last one year. The Private Carrier's Licence for those who conveyed their own goods would cost 7/6d and last for three years. The Act provided for the establishment of vehicle examiners who were entitled to enter and inspect any commercial vehicle, licensed or not, and to check documents such as insurance and log books.

Under the title, 'Journey's End. Where The Old Cars Go,' the Bolton Evening News of 9th January gave a short account of R Valentine & Sons, whose motor scrap yard was in Scholey Street, Rose Hill. The firm was founded in a single-stalled stable in 1919 and since then had dismantled over eight thousand vehicles. Many parts were retained as serviceable spares and the bulk scrap metal ended up in steelworks in South Wales.

In February 1934 it was announced that tenders had been obtained for the installation of traffic lights at the following places: Castle Street and Bradford Street, Four Lane Ends, St Georges Road and Bath Street, St Georges Road and Vernon Street, the Crofters junction of Chorley Old

and New Roads, Chorley New Road and Tudor Avenue, and Great Moor Street and Crook Street. The lights were generally operated by the passage of a car over an inflated rubber pad ahead of the junction.

1934 saw Yankee Jack, the 'Ace' welder, still advertising his talents and Wilfred Hardman at Tonge Bridge was doing reasonably well with his Guy Wolf 2-ton trucks at £245 and Guy Vixen trucks at £295. Tognarelli's Boro Garage on Manchester Road offered the new Leyland Cub tipper at £495, and in March Horrockses of Ridgway Gates announced they had hundreds of lengths of rubber for inside cars or running boards, at between 1/- and 5/- each. Motorists were advised to 'Smarten up your car at little expense for Easter.'

In April the Bolton Evening News printed a classic piece of 1930s motoring advice concerning care of the silencer. When hot, it should either be painted over with oil every two days or, for protection for some months, painted with a mixture of 3oz boiled linseed oil, 3oz Japan varnish, 1.5oz lamp black, 1.5oz pure powdered graphite, .75oz powdered oxide of manganese and two-thirds of a pint of turpentine. Two coats were recommended.

Fred Snaylam's new £2,000 coach aroused some interest in April. Built on an Albion chassis, it had central

heating, a radio and a toilet - most up-to-date indeed. The following month he acquired an AEC Q-type single-decker coach, the only one of its kind in the North of England.

In May 1934 the Bolton Evening News reported the impending retirement of Henry Martin of 41 Primula Street, Astley Bridge, as his private bus service was being taken over by Bolton Corporation. His 12-seater bus, named 'The Rocket', ran between the Royal Oak at Bradshaw Brow, Affetside; Brookfield Lane and Nab Gate. He started the service following a visit to a friend at Harwood, who said it took as long to get to the Royal Oak as it did to get to Bolton on the tram. Mr Martin, who was then a spinner on short time at a local mill, decided to purchase a second-hand Model T Ford with five seats. According to the Bolton Evening News of 21st March 1934, after five months of success, he replaced this with the 12-seater charabanc and became fully licensed to operate a regular service based on the Royal Oak.

The strength of the Leyland Titan chassis was demonstrated late in the afternoon of 13th May, when one of the Corporation's single-deckers fell 50 feet down the embankment at the junction of Manchester Road and Smiths Road (very much altered with the formation of St Peters Way). According to the Bolton Evening News of the following day,

A Bolton Corporation Tramways vehicle runs past the Royal Oak on Bradshaw Brow in the early twentieth century

the vehicle somersaulted a number of times before coming to rest in a culvert. Eleven people injured, including the driver, the conductor and a trainee conductor, were taken to Bolton Royal Infirmary. Three were allowed home after treatment and the rest detained for a few days. Amazingly, no-one was killed. When the bus was recovered and towed back to the garage, it was still capable of being steered and stopped with its own brakes.

The general activity in Bolton's motor trade can be seen in various local directories. An edition of 1934 lists 39 car repairers, large and small. Anyone requiring a motor haulage contractor had a choice of 17 and there were 18 firms happy to hire cars. Hardman's Motors Ltd of Bark Street had a fleet of Daimlers available for shopping, parties, weddings and touring - 'Ride in Comfort Day and Night.' Some adverts had perhaps to be taken with a pinch of salt. Lancashire Auto Traders of Nottingham Street were listed as second-hand dealers, but also claimed to be dealers in 'spares and accessories of all classes' and 'makers of Motor-Cars and Commercial Vehicles'. They were also prepared to loan a 'Breakdown Outfit'.

To minimise the risk of fire during tank filling, garage customers were asked to 'Extinguish Oil and Gas and Electric Lights' and 'Switch off the Engine'. Many vehicles had scuttle-mounted petrol tanks and a filler directly over the bonnet, a hazardous arrangement which could lead to fires. When Thomas Harwood of Waverley Road was filling his lorry tank at the North End Garage on Blackburn Road, the petrol overflowed and some fell on the hot exhaust pipe. The fire engulfed the lorry and its load of cotton bales and woollen rags was badly damaged.

The 1934 Royal Lancashire Show was held on land adjacent to Wigan Road, Deane, and Bolton's commercial motor traders had stands there. Trev Barker displayed the new Bedford range of 8cwt to three-ton trucks and vans. The new three-tonner, with its permitted speed of 30mph, only attracted a tax of £30 a year and was 'Complete, ready for use,' at £330. Southerns exhibited car-based vans and Gordons had the same, plus the Fordson three-tonner in various guises.

The report of the annual taxi inspection in September 1934 noted complaints from taxi drivers that the bus was 'getting into every corner these days' and it wasn't like the old days, when taxis took fares to Turton and Edgworth. There were only 15 holders of Hackney carriage licences (cars) and the horse cab had now disappeared.

Ramsden's Radio Service of 149 Tonge Moor Road and 250 Chorley Old Road was selling the Philco 6-volt car radio for 16 guineas. In October they exhorted readers of the Bolton Evening News to 'Ride to Music - Modernise your car now.' In the same month, motorists in the town centre who required service, petrol or oil were advised to go along to Messrs Bryan & Mayoh in the back street off Crown Street, opposite Whitehead's store. Another new garage, Beattie's, opened in Harrow Road for the benefit of motorists in the Somerset Road district. In November William Knowles of the North End Garage advertised that winter motoring would be improved by 'Insisting on Tecalemit Pneumogrippa Tyre Safety Service'. What this amounted to was not made clear.

William Urmston, one of Bolton's early charabanc owners and garage proprietors, died in 1934, aged 49. In 1912 he and his brother John bought a Leyland lorry, BN904, with a convertible body which allowed it to be used at weekends as a charabanc. Shortly after the purchase, they linked up with George and John Riley of Bradley Fold and John H Bromilow to form the first charabanc proprietors' association in Bolton. This was revived in 1919/20 and expanded with the inclusion of J R Tognarelli, Arthur Christy, Fred Snaylam, Webster Brothers and Smiths of

The Bolton Corporation Leyland Titan single-decker bus, badly damaged after falling from Manchester Road, Moses Gate, in May 1934

Wigan. When John Urmston died in 1922, William left the association to continue the garage business at 687 Bury Road, Breightmet. A few years later he sold the garage to Ross Isherwood. The Webster and Smith section of the charabanc association expanded with various takeovers into the present-day Shearings company; the other members continued as independents until becoming associated with Ribble Motors.

The driving test became a legal requirement under new legislation in 1935. The learner driver had to display an 'L' plate and be accompanied by a licensed driver and the Bolton Evening News of 26th January has a photograph of a 'Bolton School of Motoring' saloon car complete with an 'L' plate. To pass the official test the driver had to be conversant with the Highway Code and able to conduct manoeuvres similar to today's road test. One item which is not included in the modern test was 'the ability to, unaided, start the engine.' This covered the use of the starting handle in case of starter motor failure or low battery voltage. Walter Bradley designed a dual control car for driver training and in March he announced that anyone taking lessons in the car would receive a Certificate signed by a Member of the Institute of Automobile Engineers, providing driving proficiency had reached the desired standard. The Bolton Evening News considered that one of the most important members of garage sales staff 'is now the instructor, and presumably, every dealer will employ one.'

In February 1935 Arnold Kay announced that he was the Lancashire distributor for the American Diamond T lorries, 'The most distinctive lorries on the road and a revolution in commercial motoring.' The name came from a Chicago lorry maker, C A Tilt, who put his initial in a diamond-shaped cartouche on the front of the radiator. The firm produced a variety of lorries with capacities ranging from one to twelve tons, in either six or eight-wheeled chassis. Also in February, an unnamed tyre

factor was retreading tyres at an alleged rate of 100 per week, and held a stock of about 8,000 tyres of various sizes which were, according to the Bolton Evening News, good for 10,000 miles.

On 21st February the newspaper published an account of an anti-dazzle headlamp invented by Jack Greenhalgh of Bolton and Harry Haydock of Chorley. It consisted of vertical strips of metal in the glass part of the lamp which, being angled, would diffuse the beam of light to the nearside. In July a report on regulations for car headlamps stated that from April 1936 the beam from an electric lamp exceeding 6 watts must be permanently deflected, or capable of being deflected, so as to prevent dazzle to 'a person standing on the same horizontal plane 25 yards away, whose eyeline is not more than 3'6" from the plane.' This matter was eventually resolved with the dual filament bulb, which dipped the beam electrically.

Plans for Bolton's first Belisha beacons were put on show to the public at the beginning of March. The Corporation's scheme was for 70 pedestrian crossings at 27 points, complete with electrically

illuminated Belisha beacons. The first Belisha crossing was being constructed in May outside the GPO on Deansgate and by the end of September the whole scheme was nearing completion.

From midnight on Sunday 17th March a 30mph speed limit came into force and to keep a check on the situation, the Police Department had three cars, three motorcycle combinations and 14 men on traffic duty. The Department was of the opinion that a 50% increase in vehicle strength and six more men would be needed to do the work properly. '30mph' signs were erected throughout the borough and it was inevitable that prosecutions would soon follow. The first summonses were reported on 21st March. H Baxter of New Hall Lane, Bolton, was checked at 41mph over a measured mile on Bolton Road, Ainsworth. His defence was that he did not know that it was a 'built up' area. The prosecuting constable said that the defendant needed an eye test if he could not see the houses on either side of the road.

One of the first cases heard in Bolton Police Court was that of Sidney Whittaker of Princess Road, who was charged with travelling at

Directing traffic in the early days was manageable, but as the number of vehicles on the road increased, so did the policeman's responsibilities. No doubt Belisha beacons made life a lot easier!

34-37mph on Chorley New Road. In his defence, Mr Whittaker said he had had his speedometer checked the previous Tuesday by Herbert Southern of Southern Brothers, who had run alongside him at 25, 28 and 30mph. Under cross-examination Mr Southern agreed that this was a hit-and-miss method of testing a speedometer. The best was either using a measured mile and stop-watches, or sending the car to the makers. Mr Whittaker was fined 10/-.

In April 1935 the Bolton Evening News interviewed people who had recently taken the official test. One man said he had met the examiner at Moses Gate and was told that an estimated 1,000 drivers in Bolton had applied for the test. He also said that a pink slip meant 'Pass' and a yellow slip meant 'Fail'. The first case in Bolton concerning an unaccompanied learner driver was heard in May. Fred Wolstencroft of 15 Stafford Road, Swinton, was fined £1 and his offence was compounded by having run into the rear of another car, causing £2.8s worth of damage.

An advertisement for 'Driving Privately Taught' in May stated that the instructor had already had some pupils who had passed the test and ladies were invited. Fees started at £1.10s and the address was 'The Pike', 309 Derby Street. The Surefleet Motor School of 55 Deane Road offered a private car driving course for £2 with a guarantee to pass the official test or money refunded. They also offered a PSV course for 25/-. Towards the end of the year the Bolton School of Motoring also offered PSV tuition using a 25-year-old coach.

In September the Bolton Evening News reported that out of 100,000 applicants for the official driving test, 12,000 had failed since the tests started in March. The reasons for failure included a lack of knowledge of the Highway Code and incorrect, or badly made, hand signals. Some women motorists astonished the examiners by expecting male drivers to give way 'partly out of chivalry'.

Advertisements in June and July included a short item from Bolton's Used Car Depot in Blackbank Street. In view of the prices, it was clearly not aimed at the discerning motorist: 'Tourers from £5, Saloons from £15.' Second-hand cars offered by other garages included a 1934 Riley 14hp for £300, a 1934 Morris 12hp for £150, a 1931 Riley Monaco 9hp for £100, a 1928 Singer 11hp for £40, a 1932 Austin 10hp for £45 and a 1934 Ford 8hp for £75.

The occupant of 1 Beckett Street, off Marsh Fold Lane, announced on the eve of Bolton Holidays, 'If you want Holiday Tours without Lubrication Trouble try Eclipse Motor Oil. Largest variety in the district, come and select your own. All Best Brands in Stock. Special Bargain Oils, Medium and Heavy, 2/- per gallon to 9/- for a 5 gallon drum.'

With the holidays in mind, on 27th June the Bolton Evening News carried a photograph of a motor caravan designed and made by the Rev R Clews, Vicar of Wingates, and Mr R Mayoh, an unemployed miner. The vicar was trying to start an industry to assist the unemployed in his parish.

For the driver without a car of his own who wanted a motoring holiday, there was a limited number of car hire firms in Bolton. In August Frasers of 53 Great Moor Street advertised cars for hire at 17/6d per day. Just why the firm added the qualification 'All Adult British Subjects' is not clear. Perhaps Mr Fraser, being of French descent, did not fancy loaning cars to continentals. The advertisement did not specify conditions of insurance or miles run, whereas a Mr Meadowcroft of 10 Montrose Avenue offered Austin and Chrysler limousines for hire at 4d per mile, day or night.

The Christmas Eve edition of the Bolton Evening News reported on some new laws for 1936, including the requirement that motor vehicles registered after 1st January had to be fitted with direction indicators. If the vehicle was fitted with electric lighting, the indicator arm had to be illuminated, amber in colour and not less than six inches long. Otherwise, the sign had to be in the form of a hand, not less than six inches long and showing a white surface. Walter Bradley patented one of the latter devices and called it the U-Man-Aro. Electric semaphore indicators, which depended on a strong electromagnet and somewhat flimsy linkage, tended to be a continual source of trouble, owing to water ingress, sticking halfway and failing to illuminate. The driver had to put up with the defects as

Town Hall Square, January 1935. John H Bromilow, with wing-collared shirt, was the local Vauxhall dealer in Bolton at the time and is demonstrating for George Formby the hood raising of this special bodied Vauxhall 14/6

best he could, as the flashing indicator was still some years in the future.

By the end of 1935 the 7, 8 and 10hp cars from Morris, Ford and Austin were very popular. The Morris Eight was introduced in July 1935 and in nine months 50,000 had been sold. Morris produced a van based on the 8hp car and by the use of Plymax (a sandwich of wood between two sheets of aluminium) managed to keep the unladen weight below 12cwt to qualify for an annual Road Tax of £10.

The major car makers were in the Midlands and South-West: Ford built at Dagenham, Morris at Cowley near Oxford, Wolseley at Birmingham, MG at Abingdon, Vauxhall at Luton, and Humber and Hillman (part of the Rootes Brothers empire) at Coventry. In 1936 Coventry was perhaps the most important source for motor cars, catering for a wide range of tastes and pockets: Alvis, Armstrong-Siddeley, BSA, Daimler, Lanchester, Lea-Francis, Riley, SS and SS Jaguar, Singer, Sunbeam-Talbot, Swift and Triumph.

In an attempt to combat the growing market in foreign cars, the motor manufacturers began a campaign in the press to persuade buyers to stick to British products. A typical advertisement in the series showed two city gents chatting about a colleague and one of them saying he was 'Surprised at a man like Charles running a foreign car.'

Between 1915 and 1956 there was a tax on imported cars, called the McKenna Duty, named after Reginald McKenna, the Chancellor of the Exchequer in the former year. One effect of this was to encourage foreign car makers to establish factories in the United Kingdom - Citroen at Slough, General Motors with Chevrolet at Hendon, Vauxhall and Bedford at Luton. Another way round the duty was for American cars to be assembled in Canada and imported as 'Empire Built'.

For many years the motorist took advantage of the various battery service depots which would replace defective cells, connecting bars and terminals. This situation eventually came under attack from the major battery makers, who would, through local garages, exchange car batteries at competitive prices. An advertisement for the Exide company in February 1936 listed a number of Bolton garages where their batteries could be obtained: J Beattie, Harrow Road; Bryan & Evans, Crown Street; Davies's Garage, Hatfield Road; Clifton R Lomax, Central Garage, Crompton Way, Astley Bridge; George Lowe, Croston Street; J Ollerton, Manchester Road; H Pilling, Devonshire Road, and James Sandiford, Half-Way Service Station, Bury and Bolton Road.

The supply and fitting of new tyres, plus repairs to existing ones, were covered by J R Tognarelli, Thistlethwaites and Brimelows. The disposal of old tyres was, to a certain extent, attended to by Councillor C E Bannister, who had a scrap tyre depot in Wearish Lane, Westhoughton. According to an account in the Bolton Evening News in April 1936, the firm was established about 1931 and every week about five tons of old tyres were received and sorted into those suitable for retreading and those for scrapping.

During 1936 the Bolton Evening News carried a range of advertisements from old and new car repairers and dealers. Some would have been one-man concerns which probably closed in late 1939, never to reopen. In February, Hope Works at 29 Folds Road advertised vehicle painting. In the same month there was a court case concerning a defective tyre which was linked to John Proctor of the Globe Garage, Bolton. Trevor Jones of the Tonge Moor Garage advertised in April and Kirby's Garage, Philip Street, in May. In July, George Lowe junior advertised his garage in Croston Street, and T Brierley announced that second-hand cars were available at his 'Little Showroom with the Big Bargains' at 133 Newport Street. In August, the

George Formby in a Vauxhall-styled Rytecraft miniature car outside John H Bromilow's Bridge Street showroom in January 1935. The Rytecraft was built by the British Motorboat Manufacturing Co Ltd of London, and a number of car makers had models styled with their particular bodies for display at dealers

South End Motor Engineers of Tipping Street offered painting, repairs and re-bores; trailers and caravans made to order, and 'Cellulosing to the Trade.'

A concern for road safety prompted several articles in the Bolton Evening News in 1936. A letter from the Home Office asking magistrates to enforce rigidly the law regarding speeding was discussed in August. Anyone exceeding the 30mph limit could be fined up to £20 for a first offence and £50 for a second, or three months in prison. In both cases the driver's licence was to be endorsed. In September Miss W Hindshaw, Secretary of the Manchester Committee of Pedestrian Associations, suggested the banning of motor horns, the fitting of some form of governor to cars to prevent the 30mph limit being exceeded and a period of 'all red' in traffic light changes.

Further to the concern about general road noise, a Ministry of Transport committee suggested that certain maximum standards of noise, measured in 'phons', should not be exceeded by motor vehicles. The Evening News writer was critical on a number of points, but agreed that motorcycles and some sports cars required attention. Another report referred to the National Physical Laboratory's research in the matter. Instruments were devised for selective testing to see how the proposed MOT regulations would work. Testing would be done 18 feet

from the side of the vehicle and 18 feet behind it, with the engine revving up.

In November 1936 the Bolton Evening News reminded local car and commercial vehicle users that the windscreens of all pre-1932 vehicles had to have safety glass by 1st January 1937. The cost of conversion was estimated at between £1.10s and £3 and the article claimed that there were over half a million pre-1932 vehicles still on the road, which represented a sizeable amount of business for windscreen repairers and glass suppliers.

The Bolton motorist was also made aware of the more usual developments in the garage trade. In August a local dealer advertised Motagloss, 'A new, speedy car cleaner and polish,' made by an unnamed local firm at 1/5d per tin. If this did not come up to expectations, the motorist could go to The Car Sprayers in Lever Street and purchase a tin, or bottle, of Cellgloss, manufactured by Edge's of Halliwell, makers of Dolly Blue and other domestic cleaning aids. Motorists living in the upper reaches of Chorley Old Road were invited to visit the Endon Street Garage in September. It was now a 'newly painted Castrol Lubriquipment Station' being run by S Berry, late of Bromilow & Edwards and Vulcan of Southport.

In October 1936 the Bolton Evening News reported on the Motor Show,

listing various makes and their retail prices. Austin saloons ranged from £102.10s for a 7hp model to £650 for the 20hp model. Morris saloons were priced from £118 (7hp) to £265 (25hp). Daimler had a straight eight (chassis only) for £900 and a more mundane 15hp model at £350. For the well-heeled, the Rolls-Royce Phantom III, with its exotic V12 power unit, was available at a chassis price of £1,900.

Bolton motorists aiming higher than Ford, Austin and Morris could go to Frasers of Bark Street, a fairly new trader which advertised as agents for Riley, Brough Superior, Studebaker and Singer. The Riley models, the Lynx, Kestrel and Merlin, were available with overhead valves in the engine, rakish coachwork and either as saloons or open sports. Brough Superior was an Anglo-American car based on the American Hudson 3.5 litre 6-cylinder, and later had V12 engines from the Lincoln Zephyr range; the bodies were made by a variety of English coachbuilders. Studebaker was a pure American car, with its bulbous coachwork and side-valve 3.5 litre, 6-cylinder engine. In direct contrast to this range of powerful cars, Frasers offered the Coventry-Victor, a three-wheeler with two-cylinder engines of 749cc, 850cc and 998cc. They were produced between 1928 and 1938 in two body styles, Midget Family and Luxury Sport.

The Bolton Motor Co of Marsden Road had the new Flying Standard range of saloon cars with a somewhat rakish rear body section. Prices ranged from £159 to £299 for models in the 9hp to 20hp range, while for the slightly more moneyed there was a V8 at £349. It was hoped that this make would be a rival to the Ford offerings, but it was not very successful.

On 9th December 1936 the Bolton Evening News carried a photograph of a collision between a car and a Bedford lorry whose front end was badly damaged. Two days later Trev Barker, Bedford main agent, announced that the vehicle was now back on the road, and advised prospective lorry owners to 'Buy a

Police in this SS 2 open car would have had little difficulty in catching speeding motorists. Norman Redfern, General Manager of Parker's, Bradshawgate, is seen here handing the car over to Bolton Police in 1935

vehicle where you can get good service.' Mr Barker also offered to replace all windows with safety glass.

During the first few months of 1937 advertisements appeared for a variety of services for the motorist. A sheet metal firm, Marshall's of Noble Street, advertised that they could 'repair all silencers.' Unlike today, total replacement of the silencer was the exception rather than the rule. The 1937 car usually had the silencer bolted to the chassis and then linked to the engine by a metallic flexible pipe, so various sections could be repaired or replaced. Some commercial vehicles had their silencers mounted on flexible couplings to relieve them from the vibrations of the heavy petrol or diesel engines.

In March, Leech's Garage on Hampden Street, Halliwell, with an eye on the impecunious motorist, advertised an Austin limousine for £25, a 14hp two-seater Ford coupé for £12, or a Raleigh three-wheeler light van for £19. George Lowe junior of the Croston Street Garage, St Helens Road, offered the prospective owner of a 1936 20hp SS saloon a 100-mile test run. Fred Snaylam, of coach fame, offered to grease and wash your car at his Blackhorse Street premises, and would also garage it there for three hours for 6d.

Also in March, the Bolton Evening News related the story of eight-year-old Audrey Stott of Higher Bridge Street, an accomplished motorcyclist who had been invited to make her debut as a rider mascot to the Belle Vue Speedway team over the Easter meeting. She had decided to become a rider after visiting the Speedway the previous summer with her father. He had adapted a motorcycle with an engine of about 1hp and she had been allowed to practise in the centre of the greyhound track on Manchester Road. The engine was replaced with a larger one and as she became more proficient she managed to average 27mph per lap. However, the Belle Vue ride was cancelled after the Speedway manager was informed that, under the Children and Young Persons Act

of 1932, children under 12 were not allowed to take part in a performance of a dangerous nature. Audrey's father said he had every confidence in her abilities and that she would only be 'cruising round as the team massed', but that seemed to be the end of the matter.

May 1937 saw the announcement of a number of new motor vehicle regulations which to some extent mirrored the Government's concerns about safety and fitness for road use. From October, all new vehicles, except invalid carriages and those restricted to a maximum speed of 12mph, had to be fitted with an instrument (not necessarily a speedometer) indicating when the vehicle was being driven over 30mph (plus or minus 10%). Also, all new vehicles had to be fitted with an automatic windscreen wiper. There were already several of these on the market, electrically or vacuum operated, or in the case of Vauxhall cars and light vans, driven from the engine camshaft by cable.

In the 1930s most cars had a radiator filler cap above the grille, which many motorists adorned with some kind of mascot. The choice was quite wide - 'Speed Nymph,' diving maidens, birds, goblins and golfers, ranging in price from 30/- to £2. Or, for the really well-off, there was the Lalique cock's head in coloured glass for £5.5s - nearly two weeks' wages for a motor mechanic of the day. The mascot business suffered a severe setback in October 1937, when they were banned from radiators and bonnets if they were seen as liable to cause injury to someone in an accident. Also banned were sirens, bells and gongs, which were to be restricted to police, ambulance and 'salvage corps' vehicles, and horns were not to be used in built-up areas between 11.30pm and 7.00am.

A new name began advertising in the Bolton Evening News at the beginning of May. Harry Williams Ltd dealt in Dodge sales and service from 13a-15 Bradford Street, as well as the Central Garage, Crompton Street, Wigan. He claimed to have the largest stock of spares in the North of England. Motorists

Eight-year-old Audrey Stott, fully equipped with leather suit and crash helmet

requiring bumpers or body fittings were advised to go to the Bolton Chrome Works on Spa Road, opposite the Regal Cinema, and A Parker of the Tonge Bridge Garage offered rebores and cylinder and crankshaft regrinding. In June this firm was advertised as Parkers Garage and car repairs were added to its offerings. Whether it was linked to J T Parker of Church Wharf is not known.

At the start of Bolton Holidays the Bolton Evening News carried a photograph of Moor Lane Bus Station showing the booking offices of Arthur Christy, Fred Snaylam and William Knowles. A number of coaches were ready for passengers heading for the Fylde coast, North Wales and other distant resorts. Some time between the summer of 1937 and 1938, Ribble Motors of Preston purchased Christy's and Snaylam's travel businesses, along with eleven Leyland Tiger single-deckers from Christy and one Leyland Tiger, two AEC Regal and two Albion single-deckers from Snaylam.

Bolton motorists contemplating buying a car for the holidays had plenty of choice. James Bromilow of

Bridge Street had a new Vauxhall in a choice of horsepower, or for a second-hand car there was a display across the road in the garage under the Astoria ballroom. Southern Brothers had the latest Austin Big Seven in their St Georges Road showroom. This four-door saloon cost £155, or £160 if fitted with a sliding roof. Frasers 'Super Service Station' in Bark Street tempted the motorist with Riley, Fiat, Hillman, Citroen, Morris, Ford and Brough Superior. Those who aspired to car ownership but had little or no cash were catered for by the Atlas Motor Stores of 146 Fletcher Street. At their Bradshawgate depot they offered Austin Sevens for between £5 and £10, a 1933 Ford Eight at £10, or a flashy SS 1 coupe for £20. £5 down and 5/- a week would clinch the deal and driving tuition was free.

In the mid-1930s Bolton had at least two motorcyclists who competed in major events. In August 1937 the Bolton Evening News reported that Syl Anderton and Duncan Reid were to take part in the Isle of Man TT and Manx GP races. Since 1928 Anderton had been racing on AJS machines and he had the Southport

Motorcycle Club's certificate for exceeding 100mph on the sands. He now rode a 500cc Norton - a powerful machine in its day - and Reid entered the lightweight class with a 250cc Excelsior. An account of the Manx GP in September states that Reid, an architect by profession, completed the course and won a plaque.

The prospect of Britain becoming involved in another European conflict led to recruiting drives for the Regular and Territorial Armies and this inspired an advertisement from Trev Barker Ltd in October: 'Every day we read an appeal to "Join Up," and many hesitate, but now there is an Army you can join without anxiety. The British Army of Bedford owners and drivers! Owners are insured free of charge for benefit of wife, children whilst in the Bedford Army...'

The 1938 Bolton Directory lists 56 garages and individual motor engineers in the town and outlying districts. Only one remains in 2006 with its original title, Gordons Main Ford Dealers in Higher Bridge Street. Others have survived under new names. H Fitzgerald of Adrian Road is now Wilkinsons, and the Church House Garage is now in Bury Old Road. Parkers of Bradshawgate was absorbed by the Pacific Group of Garages and is now on Higher Bridge Street; the original garage is now Williams of Manchester, BMW distributors. Kershaws Motor Co on Manchester Road is now the site of the Burnden Rover garage (formerly Lex); the Boro Garage is now Lythgoe Motors; Richard Holden's Radcliffe Road Garage is now an Esso petrol station, and Wilfred Hardman of Tonge Bridge is now run by BCC Motors.

Some smaller garages did not feature in the directory, such as Harold Ainscough Heaton of Davenport Street, off Vernon Street; the Wordsworth Street Garage off

Halliwell Road, the Grafton Garage on Chorley Old Road and the Harrow Road Garage. The last three still survive under different names.

A car registration milestone was reached in Bolton in April 1938, when a Farnworth man had the number plate ABN2 fitted. It was the first of the three-letter prefixes; ABN1 was being reserved for 'an official car' and it was later issued to an ambulance.

Atlas Motors continued to advertise their second-hand machines at the beginning of 1938: £5 down and 5/- a week for unnamed 'light cars', and £1 down and 2/6d a week for motorcycles. The firm subsequently advertised that they were moving to a larger showroom in Newport Street and had a number of motorcycles 'to clear at £1 each' during the removal. The firm also claimed they were holding every make of second-hand spares and they were 'the largest stockists in the North,' but they did not say of what. In May they announced that their Newport Street garage was 'Bolton's Main Ferodo Brake Testing Station.' New regulations in 1937 allowed for the random inspection of brakes by an authorised examiner under the authority of a police constable. This had the effect of requiring garages to include 'brake efficiency' in the servicing and repair of vehicles.

Frasers of Bark Street also went into the brake testing business. They held a Safety-First fortnight in May, when they offered free tests on their recently installed Weaver combination brake tester and wheel alignment equipment.

Trev Barker sold a new Vauxhall 10hp saloon in early 1938 and the customer seems to have been well satisfied. In June he reported that he had achieved 45mpg for the first 610 miles, and five months later he had covered 6,381 miles. He had toured Scotland (1,504 miles) on 33 gallons of petrol, giving 45½mpg. Barker also advertised a new 6-cylinder Bedford van, car based, at £140. He considered it to be ideal for house-to-house deliveries and it had an average fuel consumption of 37½ mpg, making it comparable with the same engined car.

New Opel cars in the shape of the Kadette at £135 were offered by R Worthington (Cars) Ltd, whose premises were in part of the Bridgewater Arms at Moses Gate. (This disappeared during the reconstruction of the Smiths Road area when St Peters Way was built.) Opel cars - Kadette, Olympia, Super Six and Admiral - were the product of General Motors in Germany.

Garage Service, a small firm in Shepherd Cross Street, advertised a tyre cutting service in June 1938. For 12/6d a tyre they would rejuvenate the surface by deepening the grooves using a grinding wheel. The practice was frowned upon by the tyre trade as it could lead to a blow-out. In the same month, motorists with a leaning towards

the open-air life could buy a picnic stove outfit from Shannons of Newport Street for 3/11d. If they burnt themselves while lighting the stove, First Aid kits were also available, priced between 6d and 3/6d. At the end of June, the Surefleet Motor School, 86 Derby Street, offered ten half-hour lessons for £2 (unemployed half price) and provided the car for the official test.

Another foreign car available in Bolton was the Renault, sold by Percy Monks & Co from a small garage in Bradford Road, Great Lever. Between 1936 and 1939 there were five models, and the smaller one, with a 1,000cc engine, would have been a match for the Opel Kadette. It is debatable whether any of the larger Renaults ever appeared in Bolton, since motor taxation was based on cylinder diameter. The cars ranged from four to eight-seaters and had engine sizes from 2.3 litre to 5.4 litre.

In the spring of 1938 Adolf Hitler annexed Austria, creating a disturbing political situation which resulted in the Prime Minister, Neville Chamberlain, making three visits to Germany in the September. He returned with a piece of paper and declared 'Peace for our time,' but the Government realised that the evil day was only being

postponed and had prepared accordingly. The Bolton Evening News of 26th August carried a photograph of a motor lorry with 4cwt bales of sandbags; 500,000 would be stored in the Mayor Street Corporation Yard. On 23rd September there was a photograph of five lorry loads of gasmasks arriving at the Bolton Air Raid Precautions HQ on Victoria Square. Earlier in the year, there was a photograph of the first two of 93 trailer fire pumps which had been allocated to Bolton under ARP regulations.

Despite the ominous signs, optimism seemed the order of the day in the motor trade. A full-page Evening News advertisement for the 1939 Hillman Minx in December stated that the car could be purchased from Walter Bradley on Deansgate, Brockbank & Baxter's Crompton Way Garage, Entwistle & Walker on Derby Street and William Knowles on Blackburn Road.

At the beginning of December, Bolton's Ring Road was officially opened by Leslie Burgin, Minister of Transport. The road, from Wigan Road via Beaumont Road to the Crompton Way junction with Bury Road, had cost £105,000, which included a grant of £66,000 from the Ministry of Transport.

December 1938: the official procession marking the completion of the Ring Road from Wigan Road to Bury Road, passing Moss Bank Park. The police car leading is a Sunbeam-Talbot WH8300, followed by a Daimler with Minister of Transport Leslie Burgin, Bolton's Mayor and Town Clerk. Behind the other cars is a single decker bus with more invited guests

World War Two Matters 1939 - December 1945

When the last year of the uneasy peace opened, local newspapers carried the usual variety of advertisements for goods and services, with prices that would never return. Holden's announced that they charged 6d a mile for their four-seater taxis; a six-seater was 1/- a mile. Taxiways of 104 Moor Lane were the same, but Silverline Taxis in Bridge Street were a bit dearer at 8d a mile. Lever's, Vauxhall dealers in Farnworth, advertised a trip to Vauxhall Motors at Luton for £1.2.6d. The party would travel by train, have breakfast and dinner en route, and lunch and tea at Vauxhall Motors.

In January 1939 the IRA was responsible for a series of bomb explosions in London, Manchester and Birmingham. The situation prompted Atlas Motors of Newport Street to advertise, 'Another Bomb Explosion cuts down prices at Atlas Motors, everybody gassing about the same IRA.' The IRA in this case were the three motorcycles, Imperial, Royal Enfield and Ariel. In a subsequent advertisement, the firm used another three letters in common usage at the time - ARP, which to them stood for 'Atlas Remembered Please.'

In early March Gordons sponsored a free film show at the Criterion Café, St Georges Road. The main feature was about the making of a Ford car, and to lighten the programme there were two films featuring the comic actor Claude Hulbert. John H Bromilow proudly displayed a fully sectioned Vauxhall Ten saloon car in his showroom. Billed as 'Vauxhall's X-Ray Car,' this had cost a reputed £1,000 to produce and was being taken round all the main dealers in the country.

By March 1939 Hardman's Garage on Bark Street had been taken over by James Weir, and from then until early 1940 he advertised he was the main agent for Chevrolet lorries. These lorries must have been produced by General Motors on the continent, possibly in Germany, as the GMC production line at Luton was producing Bedford lorries, based on the Chevrolet.

In March the Bolton Evening News printed a full page of motor advertisements from the principal main dealers. The Hillman 10 was listed at £165 and the Hillman 14 at £239. The Vauxhall 10 was £165, Vauxhall 12 £189, Vauxhall 14 £230 and Vauxhall 25 £345. The Austin 8 (900cc engine) was £128, or £139 with a sunshine roof. The Austin 10 Cambridge was £175, the Austin Conway cabriolet £189. The Ford 8 was £115, the Ford 10 Prefect £145, or £152.10s for a four-door model or £155 for an open tourer.

The following day Walter Bradley advertised the somewhat upmarket (in comparison to the previous day's offerings) Humber cars: 16hp for £345, 21hp for £355, the Super Snipe for £385 and the majestic Imperial for £515. On the same day, Entwistle & Walker of Derby Street announced the addition of a new department for cellulose spraying and panel beating.

With an eye to spring car sales, Vauxhall Motors organised a nationwide petrol consumption test, with a new Vauxhall saloon as first prize for the overall winner, and cash and a cup for regional winners. Competitors had to drive a 1939 Vauxhall 10 (their own or loaned by the dealer) fitted with a temporary tank containing a quart of petrol. The winner was the driver who got the most miles per gallon.

The Bolton competition was run by local dealer J H Bromilow, who arranged for the 2/6d entrance fee to be donated to the Bolton Hospital Saturday Fund. To publicise the event, they engaged Arthur Tracy, 'The Street Singer,' who was appearing on stage at the Lido Cinema, to take the test.

The Bolton winner was a William Warburton, who managed 61.6mpg and received his prize at the Palais ballroom, which was specially booked for the event by Bromilows. There was also a competition in Farnworth, organised by Leavers, the Vauxhall dealers there. The Farnworth winner was Miss H M Kay, with 64.8mpg.

Early in May 1939 a fire at Atlas Motors of Newport Street destroyed some 40 motorcycles and other stock. Charles Terry, the firm's secretary, said that he had been trying to start a motorcycle when it

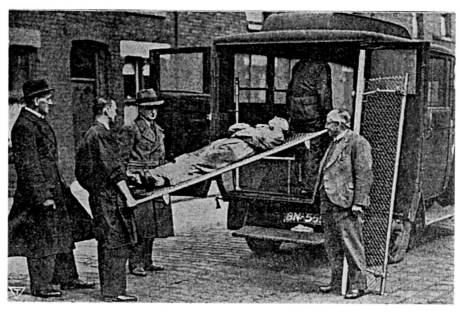

A demonstration in May 1938 of a stretcher conversion kit for emergency use in the event of air raids. The fittings could be used for a range of vans. Police Inspector Gledhill and Bolton's Medical Officer of Health, Dr Galloway, are on the left and Percy Southern is on the right. The apparatus was a result of co-operation between Southerns and Robert Mayoh, an Astley Bridge coach builder

backfired and 'blew the petrol tank'. Atlas Motors survived and, following a salvage sale in June, it reopened at 77 Newport Street.

During the first few months of 1939 the Bolton Evening News continued to report developments in the town's Air Raid Precautions. In April, women ambulance drivers staged a test drive using only sidelights to simulate blackout conditions. The local organiser was Mrs F Baxendale and the Section Leader of the Ambulance Transport Service was Mr W Mason. In May the newspaper printed a photograph of a Sunbeam Talbot, WH8775, used in a practice run for the organisation.

A section of the wartime emergency ambulance organisation was based at Watermillock on Crompton Way. About 200 lady drivers and attendants were based there, under the supervision of Mrs Mary Hamer, née Heaton. She was one of Bolton's early car drivers, having started at the age of 16 in a Model T Ford. Her father was a director of the Fine Cotton Spinners & Doublers Association and she had been the family chauffeur for several years.

At the end of June 1939 the Bolton Evening News reported that Stanley Heywood was in charge of the Transport Section of the local ARP. He had 150 Bolton volunteers, 75 of whom would have to give up their cars to the ARP in the event of war. It was intended to base them at the following locations: Public Health Department in Flash Street; St Paul's, Astley Bridge; St Augustine's Hall; Darcy Lever Methodist Chapel; Lynefield Social Club; Heaton Village Club; Deane Memorial Hall; Manchester Road Hostel for the Blind.

The use of commercial vehicles by a centralised organisation for wartime transport had been outlined by the Ministry of Transport in February 1939. A month later, members of Bolton's Chamber of Commerce had arranged to provide 100 vehicles and groups had also been formed by the Bolton Master Cotton Spinners Association and local food wholesalers. Each group had someone appointed to act for them

in the event of commandeering by the Government. By mid-July Stanley Moss, Transport Manager for T Moscrop & Co, had been put in charge of the Bolton Sub-District for emergency road transport organisation, and was responsible for allocating work to vehicles for Government usage. By that time Bolton had 58 groups and about 2,200 vehicles to call upon.

The May 1939 edition of 'The Lancashire Lad', the magazine of the 5th and 6th (Bolton) Territorial Battalions of the Loyal Regiment, states that a number of Guy Ant trucks and Norton motorcycle combinations were being used for training purposes. Some 8cwt trucks were to be provided before the 15-day annual camp in August, so that the 5th Battalion could travel from Bolton to Catterick in a mechanised column.

There were motorised recruiting drives in Bolton during May and June and the August edition of the magazine reported that a number of NCOs and privates were on driver training on land acquired from the Bradford Estate. When the men were thought to be reasonably competent they would be allowed

on public roads, using L plates. Motorcycle instruction was given by a Sgt Kelly, who was well known in Speedway and 'Wall of Death' circles. All this came to an abrupt end a few weeks later, when there was complete mobilisation for more serious duties.

The imminent threat of war was having its effect on motor trade advertisers by mid-August. The Surefleet Driving School offered an 'ARP Course on Real Ambulances,' while Atlas Motors advised customers not to be afraid of air-raids, but to make for the country on one of their motorcycles. There was an air of panic in Parker's announcement of 'Drastic Reductions' in the prices of 26 cars. Among these were a 1939 Jaguar saloon for £375 (list price £445) and a 1939 Alvis Speed 20 saloon at £750 (list price £885).

War began on 3rd September and at midnight the country's oil industry was placed under the control of the Petroleum Board, with its HQ at Shell-Mex House in London. The resources of Anglo-American, National Benzole, Shell-Mex, Trinidad Leaseholders and about 90

A coachbuilt Austin 16 ambulance ABN1 - the first three-letter prefix issued in April 1938. It followed the last WH(9999), issued to J R Tognarelli. Note the masked headlamps. The spotlight would be minus its bulb to comply with war-time regulations; the white paint on front wings and bumper was intended to compensate for the lack of illumination

smaller oil companies were pooled. The familiar brand names disappeared and their products were replaced by a standard fuel of doubtful quality and octane rating known as 'pool'. It was announced that petrol rationing would begin at midnight on 16th September.

In the few days between the announcement and implementation of rationing, there were dire warnings about fuel hoarding, but this didn't deter James K Jackson of The Bakery, 4 Tipping Street. His was the first prosecution in Bolton for having an excessive amount of petrol on his premises. He was fined £3 plus £1.5s costs for having 265 gallons in twelve metal washtubs, each covered with paper, and two drums containing unreported amounts.

To conform with lighting restrictions, motorists were told to dim their headlamps by inserting two thicknesses of newspaper under the glass. Then, from late December, an official headlamp mask was available. This took the form of a circular canister with three narrow slits which could be fitted in place of the glass. The basic idea was not to allow the driver to see where he was going, but to warn pedestrians and other drivers of the car's presence. Side lights had to be masked with a tin cover similar to the lid of a

pepper pot and rear lamps had to have similar treatment. The situation led to an increased number of road accidents and deaths and in 1940 the Government imposed a 20mph speed limit during the hours of darkness.

The first Bolton motorist to be summonsed under the Lighting Order was Henry Mullock of Brandon Street, who was fined £1 for showing two white sidelights 'of brilliant nature' in Old Hall Street. The police had some difficulty in finding the driver and he was finally located in a nearby billiard hall.

From the onset of war, the military authorities had the power to requisition vehicles as and when they saw fit. Some ARP authorities seemed to be of the opinion that they had the same power, but it was made clear to them that they had to apply to the District Transport Officer. By the middle of September the Ministry of Transport had set down rates of payment to owners of vehicles borrowed for Civil Defence purposes. For vehicles under one ton unladen weight it was 10/- a week; one to five tons 15/-, over five tons £1.1s, and PSVs £2. The cost of fuel and drivers' wages at local union rates could be reimbursed. Vehicles used for the transport of raw materials for food manufacture, or for the distribution of food, were

exempt from impressment by the Military. This was of particular importance to the CWS and individual Co-op Societies.

As more men were called up for the armed services, the number of licensed drivers for essential supplies distribution dropped. To alleviate the problem, the Ministry driving tests were suspended from September and a National Service Licence was issued to applicants for testing. Tests were resumed in January 1940, then dropped altogether in the summer of that year. From then until the end of the war, a provisional licence holder was allowed to drive a vehicle without displaying an L plate.

By January 1940 Parkers seemed to be of the opinion that it would be some time before things returned to normal. They advertised that they had ample space for 'long periods of war storage' and offered a range of inclusive rates for maintenance whilst the cars were in their charge. Gordons were perhaps a bit more optimistic, offering the new Ford Anglia 8 at £126, or the de luxe at £136.

In February 1940 a Bolton Evening News article criticised the condition of some of the private cars which had been supplied to the Bolton ARP from some central source. Another report in March resulted in the setting up of a repair workshop in part of the Central Ambulance Depot in Blackhorse Street. The Chief Fire Officer was made responsible for the maintenance of all vehicles used by the emergency services and drivers were to be instructed in routine vehicle maintenance.

Between January and April there was a series of concerts organised by Mrs F Baxendale, now Commandant of the Bolton Women's Ambulance Service, to raise money for motor ambulances for service overseas, as a gift from Bolton. After the third concert at the Theatre Royal on Churchgate, it was estimated that £600 would be raised to pay for two ambulances. In mid-April the two vehicles, based on the Ford 10cwt van chassis, were

April 1940: the Mayor of Bolton, Alderman Beswick, inspects one of the Ford ambulances provided by money raised from events in the town. They were destined for France, but no-one seems to know what happened to them with the British Expeditionary Force

officially handed over to the British Red Cross and St John's Ambulance. Shortly afterwards they were driven to London, one by Mrs Baxendale.

The two ambulances would soon be needed. In May the German army invaded Holland and Belgium and headed for the Channel ports and Paris. A month later the remnants of the BEF and Allied troops were rescued from Dunkirk.

On 22nd May the Government hurried the Emergency Powers Act through Parliament, giving them control over everything and everybody in Great Britain. A week later, the Minister of Labour asked all workers to cancel their holidays for the time being. However, from various reports in the Bolton Evening News in the run-up to Bolton Holidays, it is clear that holidays were considered necessary, despite the war situation. On 1st July the paper reported that trains to the Fylde coast were filled to capacity and that 50 coaches had loaded at Moor Lane bus station for various destinations.

On 17th July the Bolton Evening News announced that a National Defence Volunteer Force (later renamed the Home Guard) had been formed and the Area Organiser had asked Mr Greenhalgh, Secretary of the Bolton Road Transport Association, to provide vehicles on a rota system. 'All volunteers should communicate without delay with Mr Greenhalgh at 37 Mawdsley Street.' The article ended with, 'It is a matter of urgency.'

The possibilities of alternative fuels were being explored at this time. Coal gas from the local gasworks was perhaps the simplest to use, as it only involved the fitting of a gas-bag on to the roof of the vehicle and a minor modification to the carburettor. The first of these in Bolton was reported in March, when an Austin 16 van belonging to the Co-op Confectionery Department had a bag of 200 cubic feet capacity fitted. It was enough for 12 miles at 20-30mph, not a particularly attractive idea.

A different approach was offered by William Knowles at the North End

Garage, in the shape of a producer gas unit. This was generally only practical for commercial vehicles owing to the bulk of the apparatus and the need for fuel storage. The device had an incinerator containing anthracite or wood cut up into small pieces. Air was blown through the glowing mass and, by introducing water, a combustible mixture of carbon monoxide, hydrogen and a bit of methane was produced and piped via a filter to the engine. The idea was never popular as performance was reduced owing to the lower heat value compared with petrol, and there was the additional weight of the apparatus. Ash and clinker had to be removed regularly and the unit had to be serviced by a competent mechanic.

In 1942 the Government asked all transport concerns operating 10 or more vehicles to convert 10% of their fleets to producer gas and a number of Bolton buses were fitted with units in the form of trailer attachments. Then, as fuel supplies improved, the device was phased out, much to the relief of the transport world. By September 1944 the producer gas units had been consigned to local scrapyards.

Various items of legislation concerning the motorist came into effect during 1940. At the end of February, John Maxwell of 952 Manchester Road, Over Hulton, was fined 10/- under an Emergency Order which prohibited the parking of cars at an angle to the kerb. He compounded his offence by leaving the engine running. After Dunkirk, a German invasion was a distinct possibility and so to confuse the invader, all road signs were removed. Wherever possible, town and city names were erased from prominent sites and buildings. From June 1940 all radios and aerials had to be removed from cars in use as well as those laid up for the duration of the war. Furthermore, any car failing to stop when challenged would immediately be considered a 'wanted car.'

During 1940 the Bolton Evening News carried a much reduced number of advertisements from motor traders. One from William

A World War Two photograph of a car propelled by coal gas. This is a Morris 16 1935 model. It could only travel about 20 miles before a refill was needed, which would take about 10 minutes to complete

Knowles advised, 'Solve your transport difficulties by using a Sunbeam Electric,' for which they were agents. W Arrowsmith of Adlington advertised a similar vehicle, the Midland Electric, for street deliveries. Frasers of Bark Street offered a 1938 Morris 8 for £75, a 1934 Hillman Minx for £30 and a 1939 Citroen for £160. Urmstons of the Garden Garage, Moses Gate, had cars at similar prices and 'a number of cars and lorries, good order, ready for the road, average price £25.' Parkers were a bit more upmarket and even displayed an optimistic air with the advice that, 'A good car is a sound investment.' A 1938 Austin 18 was £175, a 1938 Hillman Minx £95 and a 1936 Morris 10 £70.

It did not take long for the Government to realise that there was a tremendous amount of machine expertise in the retail motor trade and this could be used for the manufacture of components for larger assemblies on sub-contracts from major munitions or engineering establishments. While smaller garages combined such work with their motor vehicle work, larger garages became part of a Government scheme for the repair of vehicles used by the armed services and emergency departments linked with the Civil Defence and other essential users.

The Bolton motor trade had to settle down to an indefinite period of restrictions on vehicle repairs and petrol rationing. The commercial vehicle took priority, with larger garages such as Parkers, Pilkingtons, Entwistle & Walker, Knowles and Gordons taking on repairs as directed by the Government repair organisation. By mid-1941 it had become necessary to restrict the supply of spares and exchange engines could only be supplied if the old engine was handed over. Garages were encouraged to recondition all worn, or partly worn, components.

The Ford Motor Company at Dagenham produced a range of military vehicles, both wheeled and tracked, during the war. There were also some variations on the 15cwt

van, one of which was the Ford Emergency Food Van. This had a special body from which basic food and tea could be served at side hatches. 450 were made at Dagenham and paid for by Henry Ford and his son Edsel. They were operated by the Salvation Army, the YMCA and similar groups and were maintained free of charge by the local Ford main agents. As a number of the vans were in Bolton, they would have been cared for by Gordons.

Southern Brothers, the Austin distributors on St Georges Road, had a small engineering works in nearby John Brown Street where they manufactured ambulance equipment for installation in vans under the emergency conditions. The work stemmed from what was in effect Herbert Southern's hobby, in conjunction with carriage builder Robert Mayoh of Astley Bridge. They designed and built a complete ambulance on an Austin chassis in the 1930s and, foreseeing a major European conflict, set about designing an all-metal conversion assembly which would enable vans to be quickly converted into temporary ambulances. The first of these was exhibited in May 1938

before Inspector Gledhill and Dr Galloway, Bolton's Medical Officer of Health.

With the opening of hostilities, Southern's engineering works took on a variety of sheet metal pressing work and the assembly of metal wheels for aircraft starting trolleys, a sub-contract job from the CWS ironworks at Keighley. In post-war years, Southern's engineering side expanded into a major manufacturing enterprise, producing car seats and frames in Park Mill, Gilnow; Atlas Mills, Mornington Road, and Merehall Street. By 1968 they were making 1,250,000 per year and also developed the manufacture of hospital, school, office and canteen furniture, all of which has now disappeared from Bolton.

Trev Barker of Crook Street spent the war years working on commercial vehicles for the armed services and essential users. Trevellyn Barker died in 1944 and his brother, Herman, took over the running of the works as temporary managing director until Trev's sons, Ronald and Denis, returned. Ronald was in the Far East in the RAF aero engine inspectorate, whilst Denis,

One of the Ford vans converted into emergency public food vans by Ford main dealers Gordons. The photograph was taken in a bombed street off Deane Road on 12th October 1941. The Ford Motor Company paid for both conversion and maintenance

who was on the staff of Vauxhall Motors, Luton, was an instructor at the company's service school. He was a member of a mobile team which visited Royal Army Service Corps and Royal Army Ordnance Corps units across the United Kingdom, holding two or three-day courses. Each instructor had a Bedford 3-ton truck with demonstration units and a full range of tools likely to be needed by fitters working on Bedford vehicles.

Denis Barker's skills were given a severe test in April 1943, when he gave a talk to a Bolton group of the Girls' Training Corps, the female counterpart of the Army, Navy and Air Force cadets. A letter of appreciation was sent to his father by Miss Isherwood, the PT instructor at Bolton Municipal Secondary School; by July that year she was CO of the Women's Junior Air Corps and came third in a testing nationwide competitive drill course held to select 20 officers to take a special course at Harrogate.

By now the Shell Organisation was developing waterproofing materials for vehicles and Denis Barker's part in this was to run instruction classes in waterproofing techniques at the Luton Service School. Following the success of the D-Day landings, the Secretary of State for War reported that 'despite the fact that many [of the 150,000 vehicles] had to wade ashore through five feet of water in heavy seas, less than 100 of the vehicles drowned.' A fitting tribute indeed to Shell, Vauxhall Motors and Denis Barker.

The Barker brothers returned to Bolton after the war and at the end of 1946 purchased 144 ex-Government four-wheel-drive lorries (probably Bedford QLs). These were reconditioned and sold on, some locally, and 88 were exported to the Persian (Iranian) oilfields. A large number of vehicles were purchased from depots in Germany and rebuilt. Many of the short wheelbase Bedford MWs with canvas cabs and roofs were rebodied and sold to local small traders such as builders.

One of Bolton's pioneer motor engineers, Harold Ainscough Heaton, established his garage in Davenport Street in the immediate post 1914-18 war period and over the years he developed a compact and well-equipped business with a good range of customers. Apart from the car side, he was an excellent machinist and the top floor of the garage was his machine shop, equipped with lathes large and small, milling machines, drills, a power saw and universal grinder, and a large capacity compressor to provide power for the hydraulic ramp and servicing equipment in the garage part.

He maintained long connections with other pioneer motor engineers and former cycle dealers. Maurice Edwards sometimes visited his garage; Arthur Morris, cycle dealer turned tobacconist, supplied his 'Churchman No.1' cigarettes from his Bradshawgate shop; Vauxhall parts came from J H Bromilow's parts department on Bridge Street; Paul Yates, former cycle engineer, supplied small parts from his depot in Central Street; George Walker, coachtrimmer of Chorley Old Road, supplied wing piping (car wings were bolted on to the body and needed a seal to keep rust at bay).

Mr Heaton had a brother, Percy, mentioned in the Bolton Journal and Guardian of 1st January 1920 as 'The local representative for Buick, Hudson and Overland' American cars, when he was trading with a Liverpool company. Clearly something went wrong, for on 16th May 1924 a Notice of Creditors Meeting gave his address as 90 Lonsdale Road, Heaton. However, he must have cleared his debts, for the same paper of 15th February 1927 advertises, 'Heaton, the Motor House Bradford Street Garage' and a month later he had acquired the local agency for Alvis cars, billed as 'The car for the Connoisseur', with prices such as 'chassis complete £375-£550, bodies extra'; the latter price would give you five Model T Fords. Percy Heaton's involvement in the garage trade had come to an end by 21st January 1928, when the local papers reported a fine of £4 for 'failing to stamp cards of two mechanics in his employ in June 1927; at that time Heaton had a motor garage.' In 1935 Syl Anderton was using the garage for motor cycle dealing and repairs; it disappeared when St Peter's Way was built.

Mr H A Heaton took up residence at 90 Lonsdale Road, and it was there that the writer, as a 14-year-old, was offered an apprenticeship in April

Denis Barker (in the white coat) pointing out essential features of the Bedford OY WD chassis in the Bedford Service School, Luton. The shoulder stars on the uniforms indicate that his students were commissioned officers

1940, duly noting the brass plate bearing the legend 'H A Heaton, Practical Motor Engineer'. He was somewhat patriarchal towards his two apprentices in relation to money. He gave us our wages in packets, with the instruction to 'Take it home to your mother.' Then he put his hand in his pocket and gave us a half-crown each, saying, 'And that is your spending money.' As the weekly wage for a 14-year-old was ten shillings for a 48-hour week, that half-crown was a sizeable sum. When I was conscripted into the army in mid-1945, I was being paid the correct union rates, but I was still receiving the half-crown spending money.

As the war situation deteriorated and petrol was restricted to essential users, Harold Heaton's machine shop was expanded to accommodate six special machines operated by women. They produced thousands of incendiary bullet inner cores on a sub-contract from the Royal Ordnance Factory at Radway Green, near Crewe. Other war work included overhauling balloon and deck winches on a sub-contract from Joseph Young, engineers of Haworth Street.

The motor service and repairs side of Harold Heaton's business continued on cars and light commercials owned by essential users such as local grocers, butchers and farmers. Obtaining parts was a constant problem and recourse was made to local scrap yards such as Valentines on Manchester Road and Jimmy Green in St Helena Road.

Bromilow & Edwards, together with the Pilot Works and Edwards Brothers, made and fitted bodies and tipping gear to a variety of commercial vehicles. Bromilow & Edwards also designed and made a number of special hydraulic trolleys used in foundries to transfer retorts from the foundry floor to a point where they could be cleaned out ready for the next charge. The retorts weighed up to one-and-a-half tons and had to be raised and lowered over six feet. Before the introduction of the Bromilow & Edwards trolleys, the operation took between two and three days,

involved the use of heavy baulks of timber, wedges and hydraulic jacks and was extremely hazardous for the workmen.

Bellhouse, Hartwell & Co of Daisy Hill, Westhoughton, was founded in 1938 to design and produce commercial vehicle bodywork and their war work began with the building of canteen vans on the Ford 2/3 ton chassis for the NAAFI (Navy, Army, Air Force Institutes). They went on to convert a range of impressed civilian motor vehicles into similar emergency food vehicles for the armed services and Civil Defence organisations.

The bodywork activities expanded in the immediate post-war years into luxury motor coaches on a variety of chassis for local operators. The firm also took on a number of tasks for the aeroplane and aerospace industries. The Daisy Hill factory closed in July 2002 and the work was transferred to another part of the organisation in Wigan.

The De Havilland Airscrew Company moved from Garside Street to a brand new site at Lostock in July 1938 for the production of aeroplane propellers. During the war it was the policy for finished propellers to be dispersed every evening in order to maintain some

continuity of production. As finished propellers were not the easiest of assemblies to transfer in bulk, the Air Ministry approached trailer makers for an answer to the problem. The result was the 'Queen Mary' articulated unit and trailer, with a combined length of sixty feet. As well as three and four-bladed propellers, the trailer was capable of carrying aircraft fuselages - minus wings - and some wing sections. Several of these vehicles were permanently on the Lostock site and ready for use.

When the war came to an end in May 1945, the Government revoked many of its Defence (General) Regulations and the Prime Minister announced that an easement of the petrol rationing system would be of benefit to the public transport system. For the motorist whose car had been laid-up, a 'modest basic ration of petrol,' enough to run about 200-250 miles a month, would be made available for all private car and motorcycle owners. Ration books could be obtained from post offices from 16th May.

Some of Harold Heaton's customers dusted off their laid-up vehicles and came along to his Davenport Street garage for servicing and repairs. Stanley Bayliss, who had a radio repair and sales shop on St Georges

Harold Ainscough Heaton's garage in Davenport Street, off Vernon Street, photographed shortly before demolition in the late twentieth century. By this time the owner was James Horrocks, one of Harold's mechanics in the 1920s/30s

Road, had an open four-seater SS 1 tourer whose splined hub wheels had not been removed for about three years. It took the best part of a day to rectify this matter. With the SS 1 back in reasonable mechanical condition, Mr Bayliss turned up with his other car, a straight-eight Hudson two-seater coupé with the gearbox and rear axle oils virtually converted into grease.

Other customers with tastes in cars other than Ford 8 and Austin 7 included David Rostron, wringing machine maker and dealer, who had a leaning towards large Chrysler, American gangster-style cars, and also had a mid-1930s Alvis Silver Eagle open sports car. Mr Openshaw, fishmonger - 'If it swims, we have it' - had a vast pre-selector gearboxed Lanchester with a cavernous saloon smelling of ripe cod and hake. Another customer, whose name is lost, had a somewhat exotic car in the shape of a late 1930s Lancia Aprilla. Mr Pendlebury, a farmer, had an elegant cream coach-built Austin 16 van, complete with a continual scent of new mown hay.

A local carpet cleaner, who by some means or other had managed to persuade the licensing authority that his Model T lorry was operating an essential wartime service, was kept running with spares from Valentine's scrapyard on Manchester Road. This was in contrast to a local man who managed to run not one, but two rare American-made 'coffin-nosed' Cord open sports cars, a rarity indeed for Bolton.

In the early post-war years there were vehicles on Bolton's roads that today would be considered Classic or Vintage. An Edwardian Isotta-Fraschini 'top-hat' limousine regularly headed for the town from the suburbs. Two stately Daimlers with sleeve valve engines gently trundled down Chorley New Road trailing a faint blue haze. A local sportsman was seen regularly in his Brough Superior soft-top machine, and another one had a Charlesworth-bodied Alvis Speed Twenty, with a bonnet the length of a railway tunnel.

A large cream and light brown American saloon - Chrysler or Buick - belonging to the manager of Williams Deacons Bank on Deansgate, could be seen parked outside the Market Street entrance. A pale green 1930s Rolls-Royce regularly appeared in Newport Street, and Nelson Square was the daily home of one of motoring's oddities, a Crossley-Burney with the large rear engine on outriggers and a saloon styled on a Zeppelin gondola. Crossley's of Manchester took over the original design from Streamline Cars Ltd of Maidenhead and managed to produce about twenty models before collapse.

The taxi firm of Lucas Ltd in Vernon Street, elevated to funeral directors by 1932, polished up their fleet of Rolls-Royce saloons to convey the rash of new brides to local churches. They also had a wooden-bodied shooting brake on a Rolls-Royce chassis, presumably to accommodate the horse racing or hunt fraternity.

Harold Heaton's accountant's son, a devotee of horse racing, had a 1928 Humber 14/40, which he had purchased for £15 and which had been laid-up for three years. This was more or less the last vehicle I worked on for Harold, as a brown envelope which had dropped through my letterbox contained a request that I present myself at Hadrian's Camp, Carlisle, for Army service. I then spent three years, mostly in Germany, with armoured half-tracks, Diamond T tank transporters, 10-ton Mack six-

Bedford OY trucks outside Trev Barker's garage in October 1942. They were awaiting final checks before delivery to essential civilian users. Note that 'Bolton' has been blacked out from the showroom window for security purposes